MW00366517

"*Luke wraps the reader up in [   ] the west, climbing routes that [   ] how these outdoor spaces can become powerful touchstones in our lives. His writing is honest and thoughtful. And a good reminder that you can always go climbing.*"

Becca Cahall, Managing Editor of *The Dirtbag Diaries* and Creative Wrangler at Duct Tape Then Beer

"*Luke Mehall inhabits two worlds: mostly by day he is a young, responsible, respectable type of guy – a liberal arts graduate who can figure out how to do whatever needs to be done at any job from restaurant pearl-diving to public relations writing. But when the sun warms up the rocks, he ascends to an open-ended life on the road in pursuit of epic rock climbs and other adventures with the kind of wildlife that climbs. He becomes a hitchhiking, sofa-surfing, illegal-camping, day-old-doughnut-devouring Great American Dirtbag. A Kerouacian voice in pursuit of vertical highs as well as horizons.*"

George Sibley, author of *Dragon's in Paradise*, and longtime contributor to the *Mountain Gazette*

"*For those of us who lament the fact that, for whatever stupid reasons, we find ourselves spending a lot less time than we used to sleeping on the ground and eating instant oatmeal out of a soiled bowl while sitting on a rock in the middle of nowhere, Luke Mehall's The Great American Dirtbags serves as both a reminder of blissful times past and a bellowing yell to the denizens of the beast we call civilization — "Get out! Get out of your rut! Get out into the outback while you still can and while it's still there!" This book serves as both a primer and a ruminative tribute to a lifestyle we all need now more than ever.*"

M. John Fayhee, author of *Smoke Signals: Wayward Journeys through the Old Heart of the New West* and longtime editor of the *Mountain Gazette*

The Great American Dirtbags

by Luke Mehall

Cover design by Lisa Slagle of Wheelie Creative Design
(www.wheeliecreative.com)

Back cover photo of Luke Mehall by Braden Gunem
(www.bradengunem.com)

Chief Editor: Lindsey Nelson of Exact Edits (www.exactedits.com)

With additional editing from: Karen Ast, Mary Burt, Lisa Edwards, and
Al Smith III

Copyright 2014 Luke Mehall

Benighted Publications

All rights reserved

ISBN 0615981291

ISBN-13 978-0615981291

This book is dedicated to Two Tent Timmy. I first took you climbing, but you showed me how to climb, and, in turn, showed me how to live. None of these stories would have happened if I didn't learn the importance of bravery from you.

"A man's life is all a matter of mountains and caves - mountains we must climb, caves where we hide when we can't face our mountains."

The Tender Bar by J.R. Moehringer

"Live your life
Live it right
Be different
Do different things"

Kush and Corinthians by Kendrick Lamar

1 INTRODUCTION

This is my second book, a sequel of sorts, to *Climbing Out of Bed*, which was a collection of 25 climbing and mountain town stories. Here within these pages are more stories of climbing, freedom and the characters I've come across since moving out west in 1999.

In some ways, I feel like I'm bottling up the years of my twenties and early thirties. Looking back, I know I struck the jackpot by becoming engaged with climbing and the culture of its people. I was a hungry and lost soul when I moved out to Colorado from Illinois, and I stumbled upon a people I can best describe as dirtbags.

I won't give a cut and dry definition of a dirtbag here, maybe Google it, or check Urban Dictionary. Like any social phenomenon, each person will have their own definition of what it means. At its essence, a dirtbag lives in the dirt, out of a bag. She or he spends their days in the outdoors, engaged with some recreational activity, and works just enough to pay for the basic necessities of a dirtbag existence.

This lifestyle was one I would have never guessed existed when I was growing up in the flatlands of the Midwest. When I stumbled upon it I was enamored and decided to live as a dirtbag for many years, in Colorado, across the West and down south in Mexico.

Eventually I changed my ways and was drawn back in to a more domestic middle class existence, with a bed to rest my head upon, and a desk to write on.

Then, it was time to tell my story, and the story of the dirtbags. The more time I spent thinking and writing, the more I realized America, and even the world, needed to hear about the dirtbag way of life. There was something that resonated from classic pieces of literature like *The Adventures of Huckleberry Finn, On the Road, Dharma Bums, The Electric Kool-Aid Acid Test, Fear and Loathing in Las Vegas, Rock Jocks, Wall Rats and Hang Dogs* and *Desert Solitaire* that unfolded before my eyes in those dirtbag days.

Here in *The Great American Dirtbags* are attempts to paint a picture of that existence I lived for awhile, one I return to often, when I need to get out of that box that is modern life, and truly live, breathe and dream. So, crack it open, dream your own dreams, and experience life as we know it, as some of you should know it.

2 THE DIRTBAG MANIFESTO

"The world has enough for man's need, but not enough for man's greed."

Gandhi

Where do we look for hope, for America, the planet, for the human race? The dirtbags. They usually descend from the middle class, where they had enough, materially speaking, that their bodies could be content, but not their souls. Their souls were driven to live, so much, in fact, that they gave up all conventional middle class ways of survival. Instead, embracing another way, the way of the dirtbag. A way, if the entire world lived in this fashion, we could live more in harmony with nature. Why? Because the spirit of mankind could be fed. When the spirit is fed, greed disappears, and without greed there is enough for everyone on the planet.

3 IN THE BEGINNING: DEAD, IN JAIL, OR CLIMBING

I was put on drugs by the time I was seven years old, a kid labeled as having Attention Deficit Hyperactivity Disorder or ADHD. *They* gave me Ritalin, a stimulant used to carve and mold the overactive mind and energy of youth into something the government's system wants you to be. From that age, until I turned 20, I was a lost soul, and I almost lost my soul. Luckily, I found climbing. Without it, I'd probably be dead or in jail.

I grew up in the twin cities of Bloomington-Normal, Illinois, and in my high school and pre-collegiate days, the 1990s, our town's climbing gym was billed as the largest in the world. I'd heard about it, but never had the gumption to go over and check it out. When I started climbing, my interests were in mind-altering substances: marijuana, LSD and psychedelic mushrooms. I was also smoking cigarettes, drinking alcohol, and popping stimulant pills called Dexedrine to focus in school.

My first climbing trip was down to the grey sandstone of Jackson Falls in Southern Illinois, four hours from home, nested in a sweaty forest, the wildest place I'd seen in my "adult" years thus far. My memories of the climbing that day are foggy, distant and blurred. I remember waking up in the morning and my friend, Caleb, who had taken me under his wing, handed me a packet of oatmeal. I was so clueless about the outdoors I had to ask what to do with it.

Getting into climbing, tying that figure 8 is almost as simple as pouring hot water into an oatmeal packet, almost. I remember it took me at least four sessions to master that knot, so it's safe to say I learned very little about climbing that first day. My window into the past, now fifteen years ago, remembers more about the setting than the actual act of climbing.

There was a waterfall, maybe thirty feet tall, and everyone we were with was jumping off, landing in a very narrow pool, and screaming when they emerged from the water. Out of peer pressure, I jumped after contemplating it for an hour. I missed the perfect landing, and my feet hit stone shortly after I landed in the water. I was uninjured, but needless to say I didn't jump again.

11

Climbing culture is probably easier to study and comprehend in the beginning than the actual act of climbing. I knew of two cultures at that point in my life, the lower and middle class people living in Normal, and the hippie culture I spent my weekends with at Phish and Widespread Panic concerts. Represented in our crew were only two real climbers, Caleb and his older brother's friend Justin, who was the best climber out of all of us. They spoke of the rocks and mountains out west, and how someday soon they were going to move out there, because that's where the real climbing was. And then there were the rest of us, friends of Caleb's encouraged to try out climbing for the weekend. I knew I was there for the weed and beer as much as the climbing. What does climbing mean before you experience it? I didn't have an exercise routine; my regimen of endorphins and feeling good was related to the substances I put into my body, by drinking, swallowing, or smoking.

The others on the trip, from the suburbs of Chicago, where Caleb had recently moved from, were scary. A dark aura of death surrounded them. One drank a beer with breakfast. I don't know why I remember that more than dangling off a cliff thirty feet above the ground, struggling up my first ever climb, but I do. And, I remember the heroin.

I remember three of the others sneaking off into a tent, to put a needle into their veins, for a high. I remember Caleb was furious because they brought "that" into his van; weed was one thing, and heroin was another. On the drive back, sitting on the floor in the Ford cargo van, I looked out to watch ten police cars in a row pass us, onto other crimes or accidents.

I wasn't infatuated, intrigued, or even interested in climbing after that trip. But a seed was planted. Big things happen in our lives, courses are set, usually when we're not old enough to understand the importance of decision. Whether it's a decision to pack up in a van and go to a climbing area, attend a certain college, or put a needle in your vein for a high, the story that is our lives as adults starts with the first chapter, one we write when we don't realize we're writing a book of life.

It was the climbing gym that got me hooked. I can remember the day I finally mastered the figure 8 knot, April 20th, 1999, the same day as the Columbine tragedy. The gym made sense to my domesticated, Midwestern mind. Plastic holds with tape on them indicating where to go, ratings that I could measure my progress with. The seed was germinating. Perhaps it was that simple release of endorphins in my body from exercise. Or, maybe it was the hope that climbing might end up taking me somewhere, because I knew where I was at was no good. That night, I sat at home and watched the story of Columbine unfold, kids gone wrong, a country gone wrong. Innocence and youth lost.

At this point I was living in my parents' basement, only twenty years old and I'd already dropped out of two colleges. My mind was as dark as the basement. I worked nights in a restaurant, and slept until noon, or later. I quit doing Dexedrine, only to learn that the withdrawals were as bad as the drug itself. The cigarettes and constant pot smoking only added to my depression and I convinced myself I was sick, and was going to die soon. I went to the doctor, and decided to do some routine testing. I had been sleeping with a hippie girl I was calling my girlfriend, later realizing I wasn't the only one she was having sex with. The doctor did the usual STD tests, and I was clean.

Months went by and I still felt terrible, each day was closer to death and nothing else. Like many depressed people, I still got up and went to work, bussing tables and acting like everything was okay. I didn't tell anyone about how bad I was feeling, which made it worse. I was in my own private hell.

Was this the point in life to stick a needle in my arm? Find a new drug, a new high that might take me somewhere else? If I was going to die, and we all are, did it matter how I got there? I felt like there was nothing out there for me. Fifteen years of schooling had led me back to the basement of my parents' home.

There had to be a reason why I felt so bad, and there had to be an escape route. I went to the doctor again and requested more tests. Finally, something came back, I tested positive for hepatitis, and that was when I made the plan to run away.

I left behind a trail of notes to my friends and family, saying how sorry I was, but I just had to get out of Illinois. I contemplated suicide. My first mission was to find the hippie girl and tell her she'd given me hepatitis. It was before the time of social networking or cell phones, I went to where I thought she was by word of mouth from other friends.

I started on the East Coast, back to the Midwest, then to the West Coast. I went to all kinds of places I'd never been: Maryland, Pennsylvania, Nebraska, Utah, Arizona and everywhere in between. I smoked cigarettes and popped Dexedrine to stay awake. I fell asleep at the wheel more than once, jolted awake as my car drove off the shoulder, sending a rush of adrenaline that kept me awake until I could find a place to sleep. Rest areas were my home for a couple months. I searched and searched for the girl but never found her. It was for the best. I felt terribly guilty and wandered cities alone. It was the worst shame spiral I'd ever been in. I felt like death.

Acceptance finally came, I wasn't going to find the girl, and I needed to contact my friends and family. It was a slow process of healing, especially for my parents, but they showed unconditional love. They even supported me when I said I didn't want to come back home, that I wanted to remain out west.

The hepatitis thing was actually an error on the part of the doctors. I had received a routine vaccination for hepatitis, which made the test erroneously indicate that I had the disease. In my own heart, I realized I'd manifested it in some way.

With a clean slate, I wandered to a small mountain town called Gunnison, Colorado. I camped alone for a month, still trapped in the tyranny of my mind. I'd pick up hitchhikers whenever I could for company, and try to score weed.

Slowly, something happened, I was transformed by a culture and a landscape. It didn't happen overnight, shit, it didn't even happen in a month, or a year. But it happened, because of the rocks that crop up from the earth, and the people that climb those rocks.

I didn't tell anyone my story, I only told people I climbed. The scene was quiet and we invented our own rules, and had our own epics.

I really got to look death closer in the eye with a series of mishaps, rappelling off my rope one time, and taking a headfirst, thirty five foot whipper another time, landing five feet above the ground. I clung to those adrenaline filled moments of feeling alive, and knew I wanted nothing to do with dying young.

And then I reflected, and chose a path. I quit smoking cigarettes and popping pills. I never felt like I needed a new drug, climbing provided all the rushes I needed. I still partook in alcohol and marijuana, but it was always secondary.

There was another side that I could never see while trapped in my young mind. There were rocks and mountains out west that presented a promised land, they would heal my troubled mind and confused soul. I just had to get to them.

Years into the healing, as a competent climber, I'd make my way into the Black Canyon, just two hours from Gunnison. With the 2,300 foot Painted Wall, and some of the other tallest walls in Colorado, "The Black" calls out only to those who seek adventure from climbing, and the other gifts that suffering on walls and constantly facing fear provides. With runouts and loose rock, there's a heavy dose of danger. Still, more people die of suicide in the canyon than from climbing.

And, there in the deep shadows of two thousand foot walls, with a raging river below, and swallows swooping by, I was on the other side, with a will to live and stay healthy, climbing upward to the light.

4 FREEDOM

Freedom, where are you?
I found you briefly, growing up in the flatlands
And then, you were flattened
By growing up, taking tests
Who would have known to fail was the best?
I failed so many times I failed at failure
Wailing with the prospect that I had nothing

Freedom, I looked for you in magic mushrooms and LSD
Smoking marijuana every chance I got
Risking getting busted and imprisonment to escape a mental prison
Freedom, I found you in Allen Ginsberg's America
As my tears spilled into my murderous coffee
Freedom, did I see you again at the campfire?
Did I see you when I gave up and wasn't looking?
When I wanted to die because I had nothing to live for?

Freedom I found you in climbing, higher and higher
Till all negativity and doubt perspired, leaving just me
Realizing at the time all I wanted to be, was to be

Freedom, then I got addicted to you
And the addiction was just as false
As freedom being found in simply the red, white and blue

It can be, true, but what I learned most about you
I learned you are an ingredient
An essential part in the recipe of a human life
Too much and your heart and soul will ache
Not enough give, too much take

Freedom, I think I understand you more
I learned more than I ever wanted to know (at the time)
Freedom, now I'll compliment you in rhyme
Freedom, I'll always be searching in climbing, above
Freedom, you are the best when complemented with love

5 ADVENTURES WITH TWO TENT TIMMY

"If Jesus can't save you, life starts when the church ends."

Empire State of Mind by Jay Z

Some call him Two Tent Timmy, some Gold Tooth Timmy, while others may know him by his comedic, pseudo, weatherman name T-Drizzle. I call him all these, as well as my best friend.

But, before he was the guy who lived up in the hills of Crested Butte, Colorado, in a tent inside a tent, before he knocked his front teeth out in a brutal break dancing accident which left him with a front gold tooth, he was just Tim.

I've known Tim since we were kids going to the same Catholic church in the flatlands of Illinois. We were confirmed into the Catholic faith together, both at the pressure of our families. In junior high and the first couple years of high school, we knew of each other, but didn't really know each other.

Once, I remember, a fellow churchgoer scolded us for talking during the mass; this was when we had the freedom of transportation at sixteen, and later figured out that we could ditch church and go do the things that kids do when they're ditching church.

In one way or another, we both found the Grateful Dead. It seems cliché now, but if we'd never started listening to the bootlegs, and then reading the literature that covered the band and the Deadheads, we never would have made it out on the road, and eventually out west where we both reside.

We also both decided to tune in, turn on and drop out. Like many a bored teenager, we experimented with most of the chemicals we could get our hands on. Alcohol got us into the most trouble with the law, and the funny thing was the most illegal and powerful of the substances never brought us into contact with police; maybe because we melted into the couch and were lost with Jerry Garcia in a world we desperately wanted to be a part of.

I've never tried to write about LSD, or mushrooms, and don't really know if I could. Pick up some Timothy Leary for that. They take you somewhere though, and in a safe environment it can be a powerful experience of examination of one's path in life, and illumination of the third eye. A shame people are sitting in jail right now for being busted with psychedelics.

We missed the bus though. Jerry died just as we started tuning in, and the Grateful Dead was no more. With things that people want to be a part of, the torch is always passed in some way, and we discovered Phish and decided to follow them around.

Phish gave us the first taste of the road, and a subculture that was very different from what we grew up with: dreadlocks, marijuana, systems of bartering, art, jewelry, hippie girls in sundresses and people that smiled and talked to strangers. We would follow them around for a week or so at a time, to Deer Creek, Indiana, to Alpine Valley, Wisconsin, all the way down to Tennessee; our hair grew longer and our minds changed about the landscape of America and our culture.

I was the first to take the journey out west and moved to Gunnison, Colorado, to attend college; a town that could be considered a quintessential representation of small town Western America, a strong community surrounded by a million acres of wild lands. I practically begged Tim to move out there and be my roommate. He was going to school in Decatur, Illinois, and I knew he would love Colorado if he just took the leap. Plus, I needed him too. Moving to a small town in the mountains by yourself is intimidating, and there is a process to it, which involves some loneliness and suffering.

Tim didn't seem interested at first, perhaps it was my pathetic attempt of a pitch telling him that Gunnison was the greatest place on earth, but he came out anyways, and we moved into a two bedroom apartment that fall. By now we were both still into the Grateful Dead and Phish, but our interest in psychedelics was fading. Something just as powerful had us by the horns, something much healthier for a young soul in his twenties. It was called rock climbing.

The interest began in Illinois. We happened to grow up ten minutes from a climbing gym that was once billed as the largest in the world: a series of connected, eighty foot grain silos that were cleaned out and modified into climbing walls. We had a friend that shared interest in the hippie scene, and also mentored us on the proper ways to go about climbing. A small miracle that all of these things aligned in a town called Normal, Illinois.

A climber can only go so far in the flatlands, before his soul resigns to the fact that he desires cliffs and mountain vistas; once you've seen these sights they remain within the heart forever. Luckily, we were out west, and in Gunnison, where the rock climbing cliffs are seemingly infinite.

I took Tim climbing for the first time in those grain silos, but it wasn't until we were out west together that we truly experienced climbing. At first I thought I was the teacher, but Tim seemed to have a grasp on the gumption and bravery that is needed for climbing more than I did. I had a better understanding on the technical aspects of it, how to place traditional gear into a crack, and how to build an anchor to dangle in the air on a multipitch route, so we made a good pair.

I don't know where Tim got his climbing ability, it seemed to come from inside, an intuitive thing, but whatever it was, he had it and he was hooked on climbing from the minute he touched down in the Rocky Mountains.

Perhaps it was because he grew up as a wrestler. I've known many wrestlers who make good climbers. They are in good physical condition, don't mind a little suffering, and can sustain their bodies on very little food and water for a day of toil. Plus climbing a crack is a bit of wrestling in itself, hanging on, adjusting one's body to overcome, to fight the good fight and hang on and be victorious.

Many climbers spend a year or two in an apprenticeship phase of traditional climbing, and this is the method that is recommended. Climbing is full of more fear than actual danger for the average climber, but, that said, the first two years of climbing can be the most dangerous. There are simple mistakes that one can make in climbing that can end your career right then and there. In climbing, you only get one real big mistake to make. I took more of a conservative approach to learning about climbing, joining the college's mountain rescue team and learning about anchors, and taking many Recreation courses that taught basic climbing skills. Tim just jumped in head first, but luckily we were a duo and we looked out for each other.

The very first gear anchor that Tim ever built was in the Black Canyon. The Black is known to every traditional climber in the country and experienced by only a percentage. It has a fearsome reputation of being an intimidating place to climb, with loose rock, run-outs and unruly vegetation in the cracks. One gaze at the walls, from a protective railing, looking straight down the two thousand foot walls, is enough to put a knot in one's stomach, and some only get that far. But the secret is, that if one can muster enough courage to simply get down in the canyon, several moderate routes await that the average traditional climber can be successful on. And, from there, infinite challenges await.

So we picked out the moderate of all moderates, Maiden Voyage. It's a 5.9 that most trad climbers could do in a few hours. And even though it was Tim's second trad route, and his first building anchors, it was already within his physical abilities. So he cruised up the first slab of the route, built an anchor and belayed me up. I reached his anchor and felt my heart sink into my stomach: there was one tipped out cam and a shady looking hex, enough to make me worry that to weight the anchor the wrong way it would fail, and we'd be falling to our deaths a hundred feet below. I immediately started an anchor building lesson, and plugged more gear into the crack. The rest of the climb went slow, but smooth, and we were soon on to other adventures.

Tim practiced more on building anchors, and once you have that skill, you've got it forever. He wasn't scared that day when I freaked out about his questionable gear placement, and I realized that he felt perfectly at ease in the vertical world, while I was always on edge. Making plans over beers and ganja was easy, following through and entering the vertical was another thing, the raw experience. Celebrating it all, that was the best, and after scaring yourself silly and coming through the climb intact, well that was always cause for celebration.

I remember celebrating a successful climb of the Yellow Spur in Eldorado Canyon near Boulder, Colorado, and I also recall how I dreaded that climb beforehand. I dreaded every multipitch climb with Tim. At the time I thought he was so confident and fearless, in reality he was just living in the moment and in tune with his surroundings and abilities. I desperately wanted to be a trad climber, but I didn't have whatever it was Tim had, but luckily I had Tim.

We did the Yellow Spur in winter, and Tim was the driving force behind it. The climb went in a typical fashion; Tim would get us started with leading. I would lead a pitch, usually have some sort of meltdown, and then he would lead for the rest of the day. So, that happened, I was out of my comfort zone and scared and wondering if I was indeed meant to spend my days hundreds of feet off the ground, and Tim would set off leading. In these moments, he became a hero, because I could not grasp where he got the bravery to lead so far above the ground. I would look around, the pine trees so far below that they seemed foreign, like looking down to Earth from a plane; I could smell them, an intoxicating smell that made me feel alive. Tim would just keep going as I fed out rope and encouraged him, "Nice work, Timmy, cruising." Birds circled, what lucky individuals were we that we could spend time where only the birds did. The rock at Eldo was almost psychedelic in itself, and I remember striking yellow lichen on maroon walls.

I remember following Tim for a few pitches, and finally we came to a knife ridge, that was probably ridiculously easy, but dropped down on both sides, with hundreds of feet of air beneath. I sent him to go first, and he completed it with ease, no protection, just me feeding the rope out as he leisurely crossed this void. He belayed me over, and then we made a major mistake, like beginners often do, taking the path of most resistance, instead of the least. Instead of making a few rappels down the face to the base of the climb, we hiked and hiked down a snowy gully, in the dark, without headlamps. One of those descents where a fall would have turned us into another story of lost young climbers that made a common mistake and got hurt where so many seem to get hurt, in the famous Eldo canyon. We had some sort of luck on our side, and freezing, but feeling very alive, we arrived back at Tim's little purple Ford truck, intact.

We had more winter climbing adventures; we weren't really alpine climbers, but we would get ideas in our head looking at magazines and guidebooks, and we just couldn't wait until spring. Memories filled with climbing at our home crag, Taylor Canyon, climbing 5.6 to 5.8 routes with a foot of snow on belay ledges; out there sealing our fate as climbers.

When that spring rolled around, I was still scared of everything that related to being a couple hundred feet above the ground, but I still kept talking about ideas in the nighttime, and Tim insisted we follow through. I suppose I owe him everything for that; a young man has to be brave in one way or another, or he is destined to live a life that he does not want to, as I believe many Americans do. They have these passions and urges deep inside, that come alive when they are ten beers deep, or watching a thrilling movie, or when they see that woman who sends butterflies to places so deep he never knew they existed. Tim kept that place alive within me, because he didn't only talk the talk of climbing, he led the climb, and he did it with grace and style.

Of course, any young climber in Colorado will make his way to the desert, to the red rocks that start in Western Colorado, and seem to go forever through Utah. We were a team of three this time, with our wide eyed companion Jerid, who was also teaching me about being brave and facing fear, and would have been a team of four with Jerid's best friend, Josh, but he was on house arrest, and he wished us well from his Grand Junction home when we stopped by to say hello on our way out. His eyes reflected a longing to go, but a feeling that he would be in our position some day, as he was only serving a short sentence.

We drove that spring evening into the night and to the River Road, just outside of Moab, where there are many towers. There was a moon, not a full moon, but enough to see the silhouettes in the night. Around a bend, while we were looking for a place to camp out for the night, appeared a striking tower, almost a beacon, a lighthouse of sorts, "Let's climb that thing," one of us said. It was Castleton Tower.

Well, there was a campsite by it, so we camped there, and after searching through Jerid's newly purchased guidebook we discovered there was a 5.9 chimney climb up the thing. We were experienced enough now to know that 5.9 could be hard, and, for that matter a 5.9 chimney should be hard. I wanted nothing to do with leading, but, of course, Tim was up for the challenge, even though we had only a #4

Camalot as our biggest piece, and none of us had much experience climbing towers.

I quickly opted to lead the easiest pitches on the route, leaving the more difficult ones for Jerid and Tim. The climb started with a 5.6 chimney, and I nervously scurried up. Castle Valley is perched just east of the La Sal Mountains, and in the spring they are still covered in snow, making for a dramatic backdrop for the red rock towers. Again I felt so out of my element, and wondered how my life suddenly became so intertwined with rock climbing. I finished the pitch and brought the homies up, and Jerid set off on the next pitch, a tricky and wide 5.8 that he wormed his way up with grace, placing our meager selection of cams, and wiggling some hexes in.

The wide chimney pitch was next, and, of course, we sent Tim up. He wiggled his way in the thing, barely placing any gear, fearlessly. Though we were only a few pitches up, the exposure was dramatic. Jerid's presence at the belay made me feel more at ease, though I still felt that all I wanted in the world was to get this damn climb over with and be back on the ground.

Tim's execution of the chimney pitch was impressive. He'd never climbed on sandstone before, and had only been rock climbing for less than a year, all on granite. Climbing sandstone is another art form, while granite is mostly solid, sandstone cannot be trusted as much, and begs one to be more delicate. As Tim progressed on the pitch Jerid and I just looked at each other, and we knew on any climb Tim was the secret weapon.

Standing on top of a tower means that the physical challenges are over. All there is to do then is embrace the landscape, see the lone raven flying through the blue sky. Look one way to snowcapped mountains and the other to more red rock, that desolate environment that is the complete opposite of a city. Take photos, sign the registry, shake hands and finally rig up the rappels.

This day, while rappelling the north face, Tim went past one of the rap stations, so he had to rig a system to climb back up the ropes. This can be a dangerous situation, and many climbers have been injured or died while rappelling. Tim was still learning the ropes, if you will, and the system that he rigged to climb back up was probably unconventional. He simply climbed up the 5.11 crack that is the first pitch of the North Face route, while feeding the rope through his belay device and tying an occasional back up knot. There is a sinking feeling when your partner is below and you really don't know what's going on down there. But as soon as Jerid and I were really worried, Tim appeared with one of those mile long gazes, and we were relieved.

Walking back down off the tower, it became dark, so we stumbled and stumbled till we were back at camp; out of water and dehydrated, but we had survived another adventure. The stars were the landscape now, and just as the expansive desert quickly makes one realize we are living out our lives in an environment that most don't, the nighttime sky reminded us that we were living lives of adventure.

Stopping back in Grand Junction, Josh was jealous, but inspired by our climb. He had that look in his eyes, that fire, that one often sees in a climber in their younger twenties, the knowing nothing else in the horizontal life could match the intoxicating intensity of the vertical world. We told him all the details and he pined for climbing with a desire that made us feel what he was feeling.

Tim and I were planning our first trip to Yosemite when we got the news from Jerid. He told me to make sure that I was sitting down. Josh had been killed in a motorcycle accident.

We travelled up to Grand Junction for the funeral. Although Tim had only met Josh that one time he came with as well. I remember Josh's mother hugging us intensely. We heard stories about Josh, the most memorable being that he had to do some community service at a church and climbed up into crevices of the old church that needed to be cleaned out, and no one else dared to do so. I imagined him spread eagle in a chimney way up, with a nun or someone looking on, giving him instructions of what to do.

How we felt for Jerid. We'd only known Josh briefly. I imagined losing Tim, and I could not fathom it. I remember crying for Josh every time I was alone for a week after.

I was depressed and would have probably bailed on the Yosemite trip if it weren't for Tim. He wasn't having any of that, and just a week after Josh died we set sail for Yosemite in the purple truck. Crossing the desert to The Valley was sublime. I think, in those days, I enjoyed the adventures in the truck just as much as the climbing.

Everything was new. Many Americans only see the desolate west of Highway 50 in movies. Caffeine and weed kept us burning, and we rolled into Yosemite very early in the morning, haggard and tired, or at least I was.

I've never seen a look of focus and fire in anyone's eyes before we arrived in Yosemite for the first time. This is an important first for the rock climber, seeing the famous walls that your eyes have only witnessed in photographs and film. El Capitan, you know it when your eyes are upon it. There is no questioning what you're looking at, it's The Captain, and I knew at that moment how far I had to go as a climber. In some way, like looking down the guardrail into the Black Canyon, I wanted to go back home and forget about climbing.

The look in Tim's eyes. It was piercing. This array of granite walls and towers, amongst the gigantic towering pine trees, reflected through the fire of his soul, and he had arrived exactly where he was supposed to be at that juncture in life, and he was meant to climb these walls. That look was enough for me to know that I would again get through another adventure, if only through Tim's burning desire.

I felt the pressure mounting, and Tim insisted we climb something that very day upon arriving. We decided to go for a climb called Braille Book, a 5.8 way up a gully in the Cathedrals. Hiking up the hill after many hours in the car felt brutal, and the granite walls that surrounded us gave me a sinking feeling that I was already in over my head, even as we hiked for our warmup climb.

As we arrived to the climb, we realized that there was already a party on the route, a common occurrence for any popular climb in Yosemite. We sat back where the party could not see us, and figured we'd just wait and get on the route when they were a ways up. I was always secretly relieved when something slowed Tim down, weather, other people on the route, not being able to find the route; these were all blessings in disguise for me not wanting to face my fears.

The scene that unfolded on Braille Book was something we still talk about to this day. The party was two guys who seemed more out of their element than I did; they climbed very slowly and made commands every time they placed a piece of gear, "point" the leader would say as he put something into the crack, "point" the belayer would reply. They were wearing camouflage shirts and pants, and had apparently received some sort of training for climbing in the military. We started to giggle at their ridiculousness, and a wave of relief came over me. I wasn't the worst or most scared climber in Yosemite; their progress was so incredibly slow that those guys might still be up there to this day. We laughed and joked about their "point" system all the way back to the car and got beers.

The objective then changed to Nutcracker, one of the many all time classic moderates of Yosemite, a four pitch 5.9 that has been climbed by thousands and thousands of people. This I felt good about, and Tim was game for anything and everything, he just wanted to get up on the walls. Somehow we managed to start climbing on the wrong formation. Yosemite, all the formations are now imprinted in my mind after years of climbing there, but, then it was El Cap and Half Dome, and everything else was a mystery. Tim climbed up, on some rock that we convinced ourselves resembled the description from the topo, and ended up running out a crack on a slab, clipping some bolts at the top, and bringing me up. The rock was full of lichen and dirty and I was thinking there was no way this could be Nutcracker. I arrived at Tim's anchor, two old rusty bolts, and my belief was confirmed. We bailed, hiked around some more, finally finding the start to Nutcracker, and made plans to return in the morning.

We returned and got in line for the Nutcracker, there was a party in front of us, and another behind. The climb went smoothly, though at one point I remember being so gripped on a 5.8 pitch that I had to calm myself down with a mantra, chanting our fallen friend Josh's name, along with the name of a legendary Yosemite climber that had also passed away a few years before, Walt Shipley. "Josh Burdick, Walt Shipley, Josh Burdick, Walt Shipley...." It seems so ridiculous now to think about it, but that was the way it happened. Tim was in his element and cruised all of his leads.

We knew little of the rules of Yosemite and camped by just simply putting our sleeping bags down wherever we felt like it. Of course, this doesn't last long without an encounter with a ranger, and we learned that lesson the hard way, woken up in the middle of the night by a ranger asking us what the hell we were doing just sleeping next to the road. I suppose getting hassled by a ranger in Yosemite is a rite of passage in some strange way for a climber.

Even the often climbed, moderate classics of Yosemite were an adventure on that trip, including the Central Pillar of Frenzy on the Middle Cathedral. Somehow we walked all the way from the opposite side of the Valley to get to this climb and found ourselves wading through the Merced River on the approach, a ridiculous way. It felt so adventurous though, like discovering how to live like Huck Finn in my early twenties. The essence of climbing is where all the beauty, adventure and joy exist.

This climb is splitter, if I do recall correctly, funny what one remembers from a climb a decade ago. I remember Tim leading up, smoothly of course, and after a couple pitches it was my lead. El Capitan loomed behind us, the only audience for our journey up the five pitch route. Tim handed the rack over to me for a stout 5.9 crack pitch. I started jamming up and then almost went into my meltdown mode where I would face my fear with fear and give up. I started to complain to Tim fifteen feet below me. "This is hard Tim, I don't know…" He glanced back with this look, and said something like, "It's not going to get any easier," and stared at me more intensely. With Tim's look and the presence of El Cap behind us, something moved within me, and I dug inside and was able to complete the pitch with some style. Tim's leads were controlled efforts, jamming his hands and feet into the perfect granite cracks, jamming up and somewhere higher.

Something happened with the rappel and we got our ropes stuck, but we made it to the ground and hitchhiked back to the Purple Truck. It was a European couple that picked us up, and it was fun to hitchhike, we'd rarely done it before.

Tim showed more of his Zen crack climbing skills in Yosemite, leading all the way up to 5.10d at the crags, all of this in basically his first year of climbing. We smoked and drank and ate ice cream and enjoyed the horizontal as much as the vertical. Finally our time was coming to an end, and we picked out one last adventure. We decided to hike up to Half Dome and climb the moderate Snake Dike. I'd found a free online topo of the climb on Supertopo.com and we'd been studying the thing for months. I was nervous about the runout 5.7, but I could always have Tim lead that stuff. With full packs we hiked miles and miles up the trail. We were going to camp out near the base of the climb and then go up the following morning. I remember being nervous until running into a family of six that had just climbed the route, a Dad and his five kids. That night we ate cold beans out of a can and dreamed of food. Tim didn't even bring a sleeping bag and acting like he didn't need one, curled up with very little.

In the morning, we found our way to the slabby Snake Dike. I got scared on a 5.7 pitch, but managed to keep it together. The rest of the climb went up an easy runout dike system. We topped out to a hundred tourists atop Half Dome who marveled at our climbing gear as we looked out across the Yosemite Valley. It was interesting to climb down the 4th class cables route on the backside and see timid tourists freaking out over the exposure. I guess there was part of me in that unwarranted fear they put on display. We walked miles and miles down the trail, past hundreds of hikers to find our packs at the base of Snake Dike. Now, in repose, I would like to think I was thinking about how grateful I was to have a partner like Tim, who tolerated my slow learning curve in climbing, but I was probably thinking about ice cream and food.

It was a long journey home in the purple truck, but there was that satisfaction of a good climbing trip in the air, our first real big trip together; nothing epic by any sort of climbing standards, but big enough for me.

Tim and I moved out of our apartment, and we both moved into tents for the rest of the fall. He received the nickname Two Tent Timmy when he had a tent inside of a tent rigged up in the hills of Crested Butte, the mountain town just north of Gunnison. Gold Tooth Timmy came later when he knocked his front teeth out in the break dancing accident; ironically, this coincided with his first day of downhill skiing ever; neither activity stuck for him. The nickname T-Drizzle was inspired when he dressed as a weatherman with a mustache for

Halloween; still, to this day, Tim is ready, at any given moment, to give an impromptu weather forecast. He's known in our circle to be climbing's first weatherman.

We climbed more, sometimes together, sometimes with other partners. As the years unfolded we climbed together less and less. No falling out, just living life. He moved to Oregon, which put a great amount of distance between us. Ironically, it was me who went full on into the climbing life, and I paid my dues to learn to climb at various areas around the west and in Mexico, living in a tent for months at a time, and scrounging by on the money I saved from various jobs.

This past winter Tim and I reconnected. We were both home in Illinois visiting for the holidays. Now in our thirties, a trip back to the old gym in Illinois was as nostalgic as gym climbing can be. Tim hadn't climbed much in the last four years, but he was itching to get back into it. A couple of young kids from Iowa were visiting the gym, and noticed my shirt that said Gunnison, Colorado on the back. One of them had visited Gunnison the previous summer, and we talked about the majesty of outdoor opportunities there. I looked at the youngsters and wondered if they had similar adventures to look forward to as their twenties unfolded. I hoped so.

We rented a lead line and went about our workout at the gym where it all started. I led a climb, Tim toproped it, and then it was time for a lead of his own. He picked out an overhanging 5.10. He tied in and set off, slowly climbing up till the wall got steep. He was getting tense, and I could tell he was struggling with his lead head, even in the gym. After about twenty feet, he yelled down to take, and rested on the rope.

Here was my hero, back to square one with climbing. He handled the setback like a champion. I think athletes define themselves by how they handle defeat as much as how they handle success. Tim didn't throw a fit, didn't curse in anger, he just simply tried again. And again. Finally he just resigned to the fact that he "didn't have it" and lowered off. But it was on.

We talked about plans to get Tim back in shape. He was on a break from work, and my employment at the moment consisted solely of freelance writing. Plus, I was living in Durango, Colorado, a great winter climbing locale, and just over two hours from the red rock Utah desert. Plans were set to climb again.

Tim drove out from Illinois to meet me in Durango. We started off by hitting up the local sport climbing crag the Golf Wall, where everything is overhanging. Again, progress was a struggle for Tim, as he built up his strength by working some steep 5.10s. We also hit up the local traditional crag, East Animas, and eventually made our way out to Indian Creek, the crack climbing Mecca, only two and a half hours from Durango.

At The Creek, Tim quickly regained his prowess. It wasn't long before he was leading 5.10s and even getting into 5.11s. His strength was coming back, and so was his mental fortitude, his lead head. Other friends who climbed with us remarked how incredible his ability was after four years off.

It was great to have a reunion with my best friend. Our abilities were finally on a similar level, and we had a great time just camping and chillin' together again. Something that often gets lost when climbing is recorded and put into words is the down moments, when you're not climbing, those horizontal moments, watching the sun set over the campfire, even just sitting at the crag, experiencing freedom, friendship.

One day of climbing led into another, and more and more plans and ideas were hatched. Eventually it was time for Tim to head back to Oregon. Of course, we made a visit to the desert before he left, a few days at The Creek, and then a visit to the towers of Castle Valley to cap it all off.

It was incredible how fast Tim got his strength back, and how quickly roles reversed. After a couple weeks of training, bringing him back to his previous climbing fitness, I was again trying to keep up with him. Plus he had the fire, and no climber is complete without the fire. On day three of our visit in The Creek, I resigned to toproping what he could set up. He was still going, energized; he remarked how he had to get it all in before he went back home.

Day four on, we headed over to Castle Valley for a lap up Castleton. It had been ten years since we first climbed it. I couldn't help but think of a verse from the Pink Floyd song "Dark Side of the Moon," as we hiked up to the base of the tower, "You are young and life is long, and there is time to kill today. And then one day you find ten years have got behind you."

Ten years! I pieced together the math as we hiked up. We talked about our friend Jerid, who didn't climb anymore, but was happily married and living out in Washington. I thought of Josh, our friend that never made it past twenty one years old. I thought of how comfortable the vertical world was becoming as we aged into our thirties. Like home.

There was no nervousness about Castleton Tower. I was even going to lead that crux 5.9 chimney pitch. I knew it would still be difficult, these type of things never get easy, but in many ways this was what I was living for: the gratifying physical and spiritual challenge that is climbing. The view of the La Sal Mountains to the west was still impressive and striking, the red rock expanse of the desert still inviting, not much had changed in ten years.

We progressed up the tower at a satisfying pace, remarking how impressed we were with our younger selves, climbing the route with significantly less gear ten years ago. I wormed my way up the crux chimney pitch, tired, as we'd been climbing four days in a row, but happy to be strolling through memory lane, stronger, physically and mentally, than I was when I was twenty two.

No one was around that day; we had the whole expanse to ourselves. The summit provided the view that it always does, the same view that it did ten years ago, but our eyes were different. I looked over to my companion, my best friend in life, the one I owe my climbing existence to, the one who showed me how to live, through climbing.

We rigged our rappel, made it back down to the ground safely and walked back to camp as we talked about returning to various routes in the vertical world together, again and again.

This piece was originally published in The Climbing Zine, Volume 3.

---

6 BEN FRANKLYN, THE GUY ON THE BIKE

I didn't think much of it, a large man on the side of Highway 50, rolling along on what appeared to be skis with wheels on them. I figured it must be a common training tool for Colorado skiers. I'd just moved to Gunnison and I didn't know what was normal there and what wasn't. There was nothing 'normal' about Benjamin Franklyn Wynn III.

A couple months later, driving down Monarch Pass, sixty miles east of Gunny, twisting and turning my car through the curves that are a challenge sometimes to drive, there he is again, on a bike powering up the hill. Where did he come from?

His bike was neon yellow with large padded handlebars. He wore large dark sunglasses and looked like he was in a zone, a trance, like this was what he was born to do. *He must be some sort of extreme athlete*, I thought to myself.

"He's training for the Olympics," someone told me at a house party in Gunny. "He's a boxer," the person followed with.

"I heard he used to play football for Western State," another person added.

The big black man who I started seeing all the time, riding around Gunnison and the surrounding highways in every direction, was the topic of many conversations. Everyone seemed to know something about him. But that something usually sounded more like myth than fact. I was fascinated by the "guy on the bike" they called Ben Franklin, could that be his real name?

I quickly learned two things about Gunnison, which, after living there for only a few months I was proud to call home. One, people were passionately involved in outdoor pursuits. Two, they liked to dress up in costumes, for holidays and just anytime for the fun of it.

Ben was a perfect example of a citizen in this funky little town. When I would see him riding around town, his typical outfit seemed like a costume, an outfit that highlighted his uniqueness. Many times he would wear a sport coat while riding his decked out bicycle. And he wore a ridiculous looking visor that stuck straight out two feet. It was neon pink. He wore the dark sunglasses and always had that focused expression on his face.

It goes without saying he had passion for the outdoors. I'd see him further outside of Gunnison than any other local road biker. His "road bike" was the same one he used as his town bike, a heavy looking model that probably weighed four times as much as the average road bike.

Friends told me that Ben figured he would make a million dollars selling the extra long visors. One day while typing away at the college computers I heard a loud voice yapping away to God-knows-who on the other line. He was talking a mile a minute in an infomercial salesmen-like manner. I poked my head up from my computer. It was Ben. He was trying to sell someone on the visors. He was talking as loud as he could with no regard for the fifty some college students working in the same room. I looked at the person next to me and gave a smile. He went on for fifteen minutes saying things like, "Yes, oh yes this is a great invention, you see these visors…I can have a couple thousand made real soon, oh yes, oh yes," he'd go on and on.

Discussing Ben Franklyn soon became a popular pastime. He was odd and mysterious and everyone had a "guy on the bike" story. The Gunnison Valley is rich with hardcore athletes: people who've climbed Everest, ski stars, cutting edge rock climbers, kayakers, and mountain bikers, many who are at the top of their sports. But I'd be willing to bet in his prime Ben Wynn was better known than any of the famous athletes there. He had a presence that justified his mysterious reputation. He was always somewhere and since he was so unique he was just plain fun to talk about. This wasn't gossip though, everyone suspected he was a bit on the crazy side, but still had respect for him.

"He's not crazy, I know that much," Bennett said in a defensive manner.

I was visiting him in his Austin, Texas home. He'd just moved there from the Gunnison Valley. After a beer, we started reminiscing about our college days in Gunnison. Ben quickly came up. He was a neighbor of Bennett's. A thousand miles away, with six years of experiences to reflect upon, Bennett found, in his mind, one of the greatest characters of his former home.

It's hard to explain why we talked of Ben so often. He was a living legend, a character so out there. He was doing his own thing and seemed to have no regard for what people thought. In some way we saw in him what we wanted to be. Someone who had plenty of time to do what they loved, for him riding his bike, and also to live free of caring if you were judged for, say, wearing wild outfits and pitching crazy ideas.

After returning from a winter away from Gunnison I was pleased to see Ben around again. He was still always on his bike, and talking wild ideas to whoever would listen. At a potluck one night, the topic of conversation was, "Who is the most recognizable character in Gunnison?"

Of course, we brought up Ben and everyone agreed. One girl was just visiting and we told her all about him. But she would never get to see him.

That night after the potluck back at my house, we were sipping beers. My friend Scott asked if we had heard, "Ben Franklyn passed away."

We all put our heads down and sipped our beers again. The sadness of death sinking in, Scott spoke again, "He had a brain tumor."

None of us ever knew this. When Scott said this it changed the mood.

"Well, I suppose he's in a better place," we agreed.

Everyone agreed and we made a toast to Ben.

In the paper that week there was an obituary along with a headline on the front page that read: Gunnison Enigma Passes On. There was a small picture of a beautiful piece of artwork that he crafted. He was an artist too. Many of the items in his art were recycled from things saved from the trash. A dumpster diver! I had no idea. He was from the Bronx and had been in the military. He had moved away from Gunnison a couple times but returned, like so many others.

There was more on The Bike too: a custom, trademark, yellow, pimped-out Specialized Rockhopper, adorned with unmistakable brightly colored pipe insulation, Ben always pushing it along in the biggest gear, sporting anything from a one piece ski suit to cutoff leisure suits.

And another Ben routine that I didn't know about was that it was common to witness him running up to Crested Butte, thirty miles away, only to run home backwards, "It balances the muscles," he would say.

"Thanks to Ben, Gunnison is a better place," Renee Brown of Gunnison County Human Services added.

I didn't know Ben Wynn. I never talked to him even once. I don't know if I could have communicated to him how he represented Gunnison, freedom and individuality to me. I think the fact that I didn't know him made me idealize who he was. One person I talked to said that Ben definitely had a rougher, meaner side. But who says after someone has died it's wrong to only remember the good qualities of the person?

Shortly after he passed he was there in a dream. He wasn't there to speak to me, it was just him on his bike, on the road, in a trance.

It makes me sad that Ben won't be way out there on the highway, on his roller skis, running, or on his bike, making normal travelers in vehicles wonder *why*?

I'll keep thinking about why he was so far out there. For now I hope his spirit is even more out there. In a space with freedom and creativity, somewhere where the highway leads to a place that is a mystery to all of us that are still living.

This piece was originally published in the Gunnison Valley Journal, eighth edition.

7 DIRTBAGS IN LOVE
written with Rose Hill

*"Life's not a bitch
Life is a beautiful woman"*

Daylight by Aesop Rock

In a world that had lost its way, we sat together at a cliff. It was just the two of us, there, at that moment. Our other friends, the others in the tribe, they were just around the corner, still climbing on the red rocks. We sat together, intertwined, as we shared a beer. Our love was just beginning, yet comfortable enough to know that, here, exactly where we were at this moment, was everywhere we ever wanted to be, as we sat silently, watching the sun set.

Her love and comfort was unexplainable, the greatest thing I'd ever known. As they say, the best things in life are free. I hoped she felt the same about me, and by the way she opened her lips to kiss, it was enough of a hint for me to believe she did.

The sunset was dramatic, first a hint of orange and red, and then a dominating pink across the sky. Crimson cliffs and towers loomed in the distance, and an occasional bird flew by. I looked at her face and then kissed her lips. I knew at that moment nothing could ever compare to this, or what this was building toward at least. So I remained in the moment and kissed her again.

I loved him then, and I had a feeling I would love him forever. Thank God I'd finally found a good, honest rock climbing man. The males in mountain town culture are diamonds in the rough. I was happy to be growing older, and to be meeting older men. We grew together that evening when we sealed our love in our beloved red rock desert.

New love is perhaps the greatest thrill in life. I'd loved and lost many times before this man, and there was the possibility in my mind that this rollercoaster cycle would continue for my entire life. Then here he was, this lover, yogi, dirtbag, all rolled up in a package that seemed to be just for me.

But this sunset, in some ways, I wished we could just become one with it, and go where it was going. We were new lovers, but in our thirties experienced enough to know sustaining love was a greater challenge than any climb we might attempt together. We had new love, in an old world, a world that needed love more than anything else.

Our friends hiked around the corner to find us content and in love. I would have never thought of it like that then, love is a bold proclamation, but now I know it was love, and I know we were content and in the moment. The group, two other couples that had been couples for some time now, gave us a look of happiness, contentment, even a hint of jealously at our newfound love. Spiritual seekers of love are always waiting for this moment, to establish a connection of the divine in the outdoor world, a moment that berths hope to every dream that is still alive in one's heart.

Just like that the sun was setting further down, the red and pink went away and a purple hue hung on briefly. We packed up our backpacks as we hiked down the cliff, weaving and turning down the red rocks and dirt, dirtbags in love.

8 LIVING A DREAM, OR A VIGOROUS KIND OF LONELINESS

Gunnison, you've taken me from twenty to thirty.

When I think back, I remember the tears, so many they could fill up the Blue Mesa. The joy, all the joy in Gunnison days and nights, it sends a tingle up my spine. The friends, so many they give warmth to our lives, coming and going, like sunshine.

I've been pondering my current situation in life, reflecting on the past, where I am now and how I got here. Looking back to a certain period, the days when, sometimes for months on end, I lived in a tent and spent most of my time outdoors. When for the first time I began to look at possessions as a hindrance. Those days were full of innocence, a vigorous kind of loneliness, and an incredible feeling of being alive. I can still smell the sage, the pine trees, the campfire, the fresh mountain air and feel the ache in my heart.

This was a time before there was much talk of the price of gas and global warming.

Before I thought much of that next stage of life that quickly follows the ecstatic wanderlust of twenty something hobo-ness.

This scene, daily: living close to Mother Earth, cooking over a fire, burning sage, writing lonely, sad poetry, climbing granite rocks and three to four times a week working at a restaurant for the cash and the food. Nightly, a fire, always a fire, except for those scary times of year when there's a fire ban. The sleeping bag, the moon and stars above, hot food and tea, and if I was so fortunate enough, the comfort of a woman.

Taking off on the highway to Utah and California, to see what could be seen, chasing something, a high, a feeling only to see the ocean, the edge of America. Then looking back, to see that what I was looking for led my spirit back to the Gunnison Valley, back to feed off the magnetic energy that is unique to this place.

Life is different now at thirty. I've got a good job. I spend more time in front of a computer than I'd like. I live in a house. At night, I write under a lamp instead of a headlamp. I no longer have to consider moving every fourteen days because of camping regulations. I sleep in a room, and instead of rising with the sun I awaken by an alarm clock on my cell phone. When the stars align, I sleep next to a woman under the covers.

In many ways my existence is geared toward success, rather than simply being in the moment and exploring the simple life. I want my efforts to produce something. Perhaps it's all those days of doing nothing but talking about doing things, something that plagues many of us in our twenties.

Primarily, what I produce is writing for publication. My brain operates as if it is always preparing and writing stories. My ego is rarely satisfied for long with my results. My heart yearns for the simple things: love, friendship, health, which aren't found through that word we call success.

Many of the stories I tell in my personal writing happened, or were inspired by my carefree vagabond, gypsy days; the other, seldom told stories of America, but as important to our culture as the stock market or homeland security. The America nearly everyone wants to know, but few take the risk and time to see.

I'd be lying if I said there isn't a fear that I'll lose the pulse of this America. That amongst all the emails, the time in an office, I'll become used to this way of life and forget this culture that has made me who I am today.

So, I strive to be close to the youth, to nature, to love, to the road, even if those dollar a gallon gas days are over, and taking off to California on a whim is harder to do.

But, for sure, the gypsy days are done, for now. The loneliness and desperation of the road have led me back home, to Sunny Gunny.

The wicked wind of the night has led me out of a tent, into a house. Days dirty led me to a shower.

Tonight I'll only see the stars if I look out my bedroom window.

Ten years in the Gunnison Valley. There are certain moments we all look back to, that guide our future and make us hold certain times close to our hearts.

Nothing is finer than making love in the outdoors.

Nothing is lonelier than watching bad television in a comfortable home.

There's a middle ground in Gunnison that I'm looking for and many others are too. Not quite baring your naked soul to the cold chill of the winter night, but not so comfortable and stagnant that you become one of the millions in the modern world numb to the miracle that is life.

Somewhere between twenty and thirty, as the sun sets and the mind has time to reflect.

As you kiss your lover, before you pull away, where you stop, and your mind stops, where you weave into all of existence.

Living in the moment. One that will someday be a brilliant memory.

Forgetting that you are twenty, or forty, or ninety years old, living the dream in a place called the Gunnison Valley.

This piece was originally published in the Gunnison Valley as Basecamp zine.

9 THE PAINTED WALL

It is like any other start to a day of climbing in the Black Canyon. Dave and I are up before the sun, throwing down coffee and a quick breakfast, and assembling all the hardware needed for the day's climb.

We gently descend down the Cruise Gully, careful not to dislodge any loose rocks, with thoughts that some climbers could be below us. Though our start was early, so early it seemed we might be the first people awake on the planet, we hear other climbers clinking and clankering around in camp before us.

Setting up the first rappel, we hear a group just behind us. We both reach the base of the climb near the same time. The sun has finally risen, and we look up to 1,600 feet of granite above us. Looking down is the Gunnison River, frothy and green.

We strike up a friendly conversation with the other group of climbers. One of them is from Durango, Colorado, where I am about to move to from Gunnison. The duo seems to be eager to get on the wall, so we agree to let them go first, as the climb we are about to do shares the first pitch with theirs.

The climb, The Cruise, is going fantastically well. We end up climbing a little faster than the other party, and are ahead of them when the two climbs intersect again. The pace and progress is extremely satisfying. Many years ago I did the climb with my friend Gene, and got stuck on the wall overnight, without any sleeping gear, and spent what seemed like an eternity waiting for the sun to rise, shivering in the depths of the deep, dark Black Canyon.

At the belay ledge where the climbs come back together (the Scenic Cruise is a 2-3 pitch variation to the original Cruise route), I start talking with the other party. The guy from Durango, who is leading every pitch, is friendly, so we talk it up while belaying. I start to pick his brain about his favorite climbs in the Black, and he mentions The Southern Arête on the Painted Wall, with an incredible finger and hand crack way up high on the main face. Soon it's time to climb again as we progress up the wall.

The rest of The Cruise is a cruise, and we top out before the sun goes down, heading straight back to the campground to chug Gatorade, eat some food, and eventually have the celebratory beer. The feeling after climbing that much rock is intoxicating, a high of a day well spent in the vertical with a good friend.

Dave and I are beyond good friends though; we are climbing partners for life. Ten years of climbing adventures have solidified our partnership and friendship, and The Cruise is one of the longer routes we have done together. In climbing, when you're young and you've got a solid partner to climb another day with, the feeling of success always leads to the inevitable conversation of what route is next?

In the safety of the horizontal, talk turns to the next climb in the Black. We mention several routes, and I bring up the Painted Wall. Neither of us has climbed the wall, the tallest cliff in Colorado.

Since I am about to move away from Gunnison, I think that climbing the Painted Wall would be a good way to commemorate the eleven years I spent there. Dave seems keen on the idea, and we make plans to return to the almighty Black Canyon.

The three weeks after we climbed The Cruise are a blur. Since I recently quit my job, I'm unemployed with very little responsibility. I slack off at home, drinking too much beer, eating too much ice cream and watching too much television. When Dave and I reconnect and plan to climb the Painted Wall, I am not only excited to do the route, my body and soul *need* to climb.

I gather as much information as possible about the Southern Arête, mostly through my friends that have done the route. I try to stay away from internet forums; the Black scares many a climber away, and reading about some stranger's horrific experience on the route just might taint my image of the climb.

All of my friends report that the route is long; very long, when you think you're at the top, you probably still have a ways to go. The hike back is also an endeavor in itself, and a couple of my friends tell me stories about wandering around the rim of the canyon in the dark, stumbling for hours without food or water.

Dave and I decide to meet up in the afternoon the day before the climb and scope out the trail to the top of the Painted Wall. We stash a jug of water; in the Black one almost always runs out of water on the climb.

The night before the climb I am tired, but wired. I eventually fall into a restless sleep, my internal clock just waiting for the annoying alarm on my cell phone to go off at 4:30, and I wake up several times in the night thinking it is time to wake up.

Breakfast, coffee, it's all hurried, like always. I feel like I haven't really slept. It's a colder morning than when we did The Cruise. It's October now, and the cool Colorado air seeps into our bodies and under our skin.

We begin hiking down the S.O.B. gully, stepping down boulder after boulder, descending into the canyon. After an hour the sun is up, and the Painted Wall is before us: proud, provoking fear, but at the same time encouraging courage. Large, pink pegmatite bands run through the wall, like brushstrokes from Mother Nature. Some of the peg bands explode like lightning across the wall. Other sections of peg, near the top of the formation, are seventy to eighty feet tall and hundreds of feet across. The larger peg bands near the top of the wall resemble dragons, and hardcore Black Canyon climbers have horrific tales of climbing these features.

All around us are other big walls, granite in every direction. The Gunnison River rages through the canyon; small waterfalls produce frothy whitewater, as the water flows past boulders that fell off the canyon walls many moons ago. All this wild rock scenery with no other climbers in sight.

Some walls are better to look at than to climb. The closer we get to the Painted Wall, the uglier it appears. In the Black Canyon guidebook, it is described as an overhanging scree field. In the last ten years I've been climbing in the canyon, it is the only wall I've regularly heard about sections of climbs falling off the wall. Yes, that's right, a pitch of the climb literally coming undone from the wall, adding to the scree fields below.

From afar it is a masterpiece, up close, the loose rock and questionable features are more visible. Any climber that does more than one route on this wall is a true lover of the brutal, Black Canyon.

We slam water on the approach and fill up our water bottles in the river, adding iodine tablets for purification, near the beach-like campsites that brave fisherman and even braver whitewater kayakers use. For some reason, we linger at the river, as if we have the time to. Finally, we make the last approach to the start of the climb.

After hearing stories of friends getting off route on the start of the climb, we've carefully studied the initial section from photographs and various overlooks in the canyon. Dave sets off leading, and eventually the rope comes tight, and it's time for me to start up. The first pitches are the type of climbing one would only do to attain better terrain up higher: loose blocks, prickly bushes, and funky cracks. This leads us up to a scree field and finally some better climbing. Eventually, we're as hot as we were cold in the morning, and we strip layers off as if they were useless, tying the clothing around our waists and stuffing it in our one, small backpack.

The climbing gets better, nicer cracks, and less loose rock, yet we're amazed by the choss of the route, given how many times the route has been climbed. I take note that even Dave, an alpine climber, who has seen his fair share of choss, makes multiple remarks about how loose the climb is.

We're enjoying ourselves, slowly progressing up the wall, and into a long chimney/off-width system. The chimneys demand complete focus and concentration, as the protection is sparse. Forty feet of chimney climbing without gear is common, and we wiggle ourselves into the cracks, facing the fear of the situation.

The climb is full of booty, gear left behind from a party that had to retreat; I take the time to remove some of the gear, mostly nuts, slings and carabiners. There isn't a bolt or a fixed anchor anywhere on this route: typical style of a Black Canyon climb. It's a style I'm grateful that the pioneers of the canyon established, one that forces the climber to be creative with gear, and rise to the challenge of the occasional runout.

The chimney pitches go on and on, and I sense that feeling of dread that many have felt before in the Black Canyon: *are we moving fast enough?*

After leading a block of pitches, we are finally out of the chimney system. When Dave reaches my perch, a comfortable-sized ledge, I glance at the watch he's got on his harness; it's getting late, and it's time to get off this damn wall.

Dave takes a quick glance at the topo, and leads off into a run-out 5.9 face section, completing the dangerous section quickly. Then he takes a wrong turn, heading left into no man's land. He realizes he's going the wrong way and finds some slings wrapped around a boulder, following in the footsteps of another climber that has made this mistake. He quickly lowers off this anchor back to my ledge and pulls the rope.

The feeling of dread hits me again, *we've got to get out of here man.* We study the topo and realize we need to get out on the main face of the wall, and go right instead of left, realizing that Dave was headed the correct way, but needed to traverse right where he went left. The face section has no protection, and is right above a massive boulder, above a chimney gash that we can't see the end of. A fall would be disastrous. I'm tired and mentally drained, and I can't complete the moves.

We study the topo and the wall again. By this time the sun is setting and we can tell it won't be long before the light leaves us. We are perplexed by the wall and what we should do. We know we need to climb, but can't figure out which way to go. As the sun keeps setting more dread comes over us; we're about to be stuck on the wall without bivy gear for the night.

"You've got that lighter right?" I ask Dave.

Immediately, I begin a scour of the ledge for meager pieces of twigs and branches from the prickle and Mormon Tea bushes, assembling a humble pile. We pick out where we are going to sleep. There's a small section where we can both lie down in the fetal position, with small rocks built around it, evidence that other climbers have been in our situation before, stuck on the 2,300 foot Painted Wall

45

for an unplanned bivouac.

The dread overcomes us for about an hour till we sink into the despair of the situation. Then it's not so bad. It's a waiting game, we have jackets and hats and gloves and layers, and some twigs to burn so we probably won't become hypothermic. Most importantly, we are in good company. Dave and I have spent several nights together in the vertical world.

Conversation is minimal, but Dave and I both stay positive. At one point he tells me, "Well if there was anyone I would want to be benighted here with it would be you." Dave is an accomplished climber and I take the comment to heart. Neither of us blames the other for the grim night we have ahead of us.

The night sky is clear, another positive sign we'll be fine on the wall. We watch the stars as if they were the big screen. Slowly they appear in the night. Soon the sky is an expansive array of stars. Dave points out some constellations I'd never seen before, but I have forgotten, and will forget until I see them again another starry night, and then remember.

The stars change as we watch them; they represent the only light in the sky, save for the occasional airplane. The new moon is barely even a sliver. We curl up, spooning together to make vain attempts at sleep. The sleep is not real sleep, but the mind starts to dream for a second, until it realizes that the only dreams that will be had that night are the lucid dreams of staring at the stars, and realizing you are cold and stuck on this wall.

I keep pestering Dave to burn some of the twigs for warmth, probably once every half an hour. At two in the morning he gives in. His reluctance to start burning the small branches was smart; they last till the first rays of the morning sun come from over the rim of the canyon.

We eat "breakfast," what's left over from our food stash: a gel for me and a granola bar for Dave, but no water to wash it down.

We wait for the sun to hit us, to warm us up. Eventually it does

---

and we stare up at the wall, looking to unlock the sequence of where to go. We're both dehydrated and fatigued. All we want to do is get off the wall. Going down isn't an option. We'd lose half our rack if we decided to rappel.

After staring at the granite wall as if it were a chess board, and trying to decide our next move, I make the decision to try a different way than the topo from the guidebook suggests: a traversing section, which looks like there are some cracks for gear, unlike the runout section the guide describes.

The feeling as I start leading out is more dread and fear, but the motion of climbing on with risk is not as bad as the initial dread. I place some gear and traverse out, looking up on the wall for the finger and hand crack that is supposed to be the finest climbing on the route. My heart pumping, my muscles feeling the burn of the night without sleep and water, I move delicately on decent, but lichen covered holds, every move a prayer that the climb will continue without a fall.

Eventually, I secure more good gear in the grassy cracks, and I spot the beautiful finger and hand crack above. I build a belay and bring Dave up. We manage the crux pitch, exhausted, pulling on gear for progress, whatever it takes. The rest of the climb wanders up loose sections of granite, with more loose blocks everywhere; when we think we're at the top, we're not.

A final section of moderate cracks through the pink pegmatite and we are at the rim, done with the climbing. Dave, appearing exhausted but relieved, gives me a big hug, and a weight is carried off my shoulders. Finally, in a rush of endorphins, the suffering on the wall is rewarded. A wave of relief and happiness overcomes me.

We wander through the woods to find the hiking trail that will lead us to camp. Every step is a challenge. With no trail to guide our way we just wander, with Dave's sense of direction guiding us. Ten minutes in I step on a cactus, and it latches onto my ankle. I scream out in pain, and then remove it. Five minutes later I step on another one.

Finally, we hit the trail, and after stumbling along the trail for twenty minutes we retrieve the stashed jug of Gatorade water. Dave gets it out of the tree, and insists I have the first sip. The sensation and taste is better than any drink I'd ever tasted in my life. We savor the half gallon, it goes quickly, but it is enough to snap us back to life as we continue on the trail. Just as the trail ends and the ranger station appears on the horizon, so does Ryan, a climbing ranger, who is also a friend from Gunnison, about to set out on a jog to check up on us. We're glad to see his face, and he shows us to the water spigot on the side of the ranger's station.

We hop in Dave's truck to drive to our campsite to recover. The fruits of the world put us in a dreamlike state of satisfaction as we bask in being young and alive. First it's the satisfaction of water, then food, then finally beer. We build a proper fire, and I'm so tired I start to hallucinate in the coals. Crawling into my tent at the end of the evening, I feel like a king to be in a sleeping bag.

The next morning, the endorphin high, or adrenaline or whatever, is still present, a feeling of accomplishment and relief. The world is ours to be had. Dave and I discuss where we went wrong, wasting time here and there. In this moment of repose we can't take back anything; we can only learn from the lessons and improve our efficiency with time. Besides, we still felt as if we'd accomplished something: we climbed the biggest wall in Colorado. And isn't the soul point of climbing how you feel while doing it, and, afterwards, in the celebration of it all?

That was the end of the Black Canyon season for us. But, the climbing season continued. I moved to Durango where the beginning of winter was exceptionally warm, until the snow finally came.

One day at East Animas, the local crag, I ran into Marcus, the fellow from Durango we'd climbed alongside on The Cruise. He asked me if I made it back to the Black after that route. I replied that I had and we did end up doing the Southern Arête on his recommendation. He smiled and gave a look only a fellow climber could, who had climbed the route as well.

"It's a long one isn't it?" he said.

I thought for a second to go into the details of the climb, the benightment and all that, but decided not to. I simply replied, "It is a long one," and my mind drifted off to the Black Canyon.

This piece was originally published in The Climbing Zine, Volume 3.

"The license plates were from Canada, Colorado, Wyoming, New York, most of these junkers having been babied down the road with little chance of ever reaching Yosemite, and no chance of ever leaving it. And for every head in that lot, twenty just like it had been abandoned in flames on some lonesome highway, the plates stripped off and the driver, laden with ropes and bags thumbing on towards the Mecca."

Rock Jocks, Wall Rats and Hang Dogs by John Long

It all depended on the Freedom Mobile really. Gene's truck had just recently broken down, and if we were going on this climbing trip we would have to roll out in my graffiti-ed red, white and blue 1988 Mazda.

When I painted the car, complete with stars and stripes, a couple years ago, I thought that I'd turned it into a townie mobile for life. I was happily living in Gunnison, Colorado, and the car was reaching 200,000 miles. Ever since I saw *Easy Rider* for the first time, I'd always wanted to paint a car in the colors of our country and I figured this was the time: my car was old and I wasn't getting any younger.

For two years the Freedom Mobile lived out its days driving back and forth from Gunnison to Crested Butte on Highway 135, a thirty mile stretch I drove, half the time for work, half the time for pleasure. Occasionally I'd get a wild hair and drive a hundred miles or so with a ladyfriend to some hot springs, but other than that the Freedom Mobile hardly left its home in the heart of the Colorado Rocky Mountains.

Life rarely goes according to plans, and I was witnessing my life in the Gunnison Valley change. My dream job with the college had been cut to half time, and I'd just broken up with the first woman I'd ever been in love with. So I decided to make some changes. Since I up and moved to Colorado from the Midwest a decade ago, I've realized that a leap of faith into a new situation can be exactly what the soul needs to truly live life. I was going to move somewhere, and make a fresh start.

One place I'd always wanted to live was Durango, just three hours southwest of Gunnison. I made a trip down there, visited with some contacts I'd made from the local weekly newspaper and the college, and got a great feeling from my visit.

It was decided, I'd move to Durango. I resigned from my job and started making plans for the transition. It felt right in my gut, moving on from one existence in a mountain town to another, and the greatest thing about this whole transition was that it was open-ended, I could take a month long climbing trip in the interim.

For many years now I've identified myself as a climber. The simple designation as a climber, sharing that information with others, especially non-climbers, often solicits a response of admiration and awe from the non-climbing public. Statements like, "Oh I could never do that…I'm scared of heights," etcetera.

I often reply that what really scares me is not a thousand feet of pure exposure beneath my feet, or the possibility of a big fall on a rock face, but the couch, the horizontal, too much time on my hands. I'm terrified of what I become when I don't have movement, exercise, and time to live life in the wild places of the world, to feel truly alive like I'm not wasting a minute.

So, in the midst of all this change, my biggest fear was not about the upcoming life changes, it was that I would not make the most of the opportunity that was right in front of my face: I had no job, no girlfriend, and no place to live. I had freedom, or at least the possibility to live with freedom.

When Gene's truck broke down he called me up and shared the news. We'd been planning an autumn off season excursion to the climbing areas of the West, which now, all of a sudden, completely relied on the Freedom Mobile if it was to be accomplished. Luckily, Gene caught me at a moment of optimism; I'd just completed a climb of the Painted Wall in the Black Canyon, at 2,300 feet, the tallest cliff in Colorado, and I was in that post success frame of mind that climbing often brings. For in climbing, success or failure often lies in the mind; when the climber believes he can do something, often he makes that a reality through his will.

"Do you think we could take your car on this trip?" Gene asked me.

"Sure…" I said, not completely convinced if I actually believed it.

"Well alright, then we can still do this…." Gene replied and then we went on with planning the details.

I drove to Gene's place in Telluride with everything I owned packed into the Freedom Mobile. Like many a mountain town resident, my two bicycles on the vehicle were each worth more than my vehicle. Priorities. At Gene's place I stored the bikes and the domestic possessions for the duration of the trip.

In the morning it was snowing. An early season snow, it turned into a blizzard as we slowly rolled out of Telluride, headed west. Our first stop on the trip: Red Rocks, just outside of Las Vegas.

We drove out of the snow and soon we had open, clear roads in front of us, headed into Utah. Now, in my experience as a freedom loving rock climber, if there is one state that does not approve of our kind, it is Utah. Colorado vehicles are often profiled while driving through, and are frequently pulled over and targeted for what they may have in their vehicle: marijuana. Gene and I had a modest supply of the herb, legal in Colorado, but something that could land us with a stiff fine and/or a visit to the local jail in Mormon country.

With this in mind, I felt uneasy and nervous about driving into Utah. Gene, on the other hand, had an air of confidence about him; he wasn't worried. Gene's confidence wasn't simply limited to crossing Utah, he was also extremely confident in the Freedom Mobile. Whenever I expressed doubt about the car, and the fact that we were about to put thousands of miles on a vehicle that had broken down several times in the last two years, he countered my thoughts with positivity. In many ways this trip was Gene's manifestation, and I was along for the ride.

So we rolled through the desert of Utah, the Freedom Mobile attracting the attention of many vehicles passing us on I-70. At a gas station the attendant looked out at my car and complimented it, then asked, "Do you get pulled over a lot?"

"Well, actually, yes," I replied.

It was true, I did get pulled over frequently, mostly for legit reasons and not profiling. At that point the Freedom Mobile was missing the front bumper, had a broken windshield, and unreliable headlights that would only work when I fiddled with the wiring.

We drove into the night and were relieved when we crossed into Nevada. Every stop in the nighttime demanded we pop the hood and mess with the wiring until the headlights came on. Police vehicles passed by, but didn't give the Freedom Mobile a second look. Finally, the lights of Las Vegas appeared. We rolled into the Red Rocks campsite around midnight and did what climbers do: cracked a beer, set up camp, and drifted off into sleep under the starless Vegas night.

We woke up feeling good. It was sunny, and we were going climbing. The campsite was full, almost entirely climbers, as a big storm had rolled through Yosemite, forcing the tribe out to locations with better climbing conditions.

We found ourselves at a sport climbing crag in the main hang at Red Rocks. There, with a dozen or so other climbers, we monkeyed around on the walls. It was a typical representation of the climbing community: folks from all over, a beautiful young English woman who climbed with a grace none of the guys could match, a guy who talked bigger and better than he climbed, and a crew of folks that were smelly, but friendly and willing to chat and offer beta. Climbers can be some of the nicest and weirdest people one will ever meet.

Of course, one guy was a friend of a friend of Gene's, and at that Las Vegas crag we were home amongst the climbing community. Gene and I both floated and failed on the bolted climbs, the floating taking place on the vertical terrain and the failure happening on the walls, which were overhanging. However, in sport climbing failure is all part of it, and it still builds strength.

The sun was shining, it was seventy degrees, and everything felt perfect. Off in the distance, across the desert landscape with cactuses and Joshua trees, were the bigger walls of Red Rocks, where the true adventure takes place. These fantastic sandstone cliffs were split by shades of white, pink, and maroon in several separate canyons. Many of the cliffs formed in diamond shapes that make them look like high mountain peaks.

By midday, they were already in shade. Our new friend told us it was really cold in the canyons, which was hard to believe as we sat there basking in the sun, almost too hot. Climbing is often too hot or too cold and we considered his comments, but we didn't change our plans. We were headed for those taller cliffs the following day.

Getting ready the next morning, up early, with a sublime sunrise coming up over Las Vegas, where people were surely still up from the night before, we were well rested and ready for a full day of adventure. Coffee ignited our excitement, and the eggs and bacon, cooked over Gene's blackened Coleman stove, fueled our bodies.

Gene's enthusiasm for climbing cannot be understated, and after a cup of coffee this guy was primed and ready to go, talking a mile a minute, animated and psyching me up during this whole process. If a climber is measured by his passion and enthusiasm, and if I can say so myself, this is how they should be measured, then Gene is the greatest climber in the world.

So we parked the Freedom Mobile and began hiking up the canyon to the wall. The hike warmed us up, but by the time we reached the wall we were already in the shade. A couple was standing there, all bundled up in coats and hats and gloves, looking cold. They were waiting in line behind another party, for the popular climb, Crimson Chrysalis. They were friendly and from the East Coast, where Gene is from, and they struck up a conversation about something from that region of the country.

We carried on to our climb and started up the Cloud Tower. I was leading the first half of the route, and Gene would finish up. I led up, stuffing my hands in the crack and breathing on them to stay warm. It was indeed cold, and almost cold to the point where it really wasn't much fun, just work. But crack climbing goes beyond fun, and we carried on, not really thinking about retreat. Another great hand crack led up to the crux pitch, a thin finger crack, one where just the fingertips slide in, and you're searching for dime sized edges for the feet.

I started up this pitch, with some face moves necessary to get in to the crack. Cold and unsure, I made some awkward moves, bumbling gear into the tapering cracks, stepping above it, not feeling confident at all and doubting myself. Above my gear, I felt exposed and out of my element, sketching a couple more face climbing moves and finally reaching the perfect thin crack.

I yelled down to Gene, "I'm not really feeling this. Do you want me to lower off so you can give it a go?"

Just as I said this we looked down to see another party below us, racing up the wall. Knowing if I lowered off and gave Gene a chance to do the crack in better free climbing style it would slow us down, causing a traffic jam on the wall, we figured it would be best if I just got the thing done. Trying not to be frustrated with my lack of mental mojo, I started aiding up the crack, pulling on thin cams, and stepping in slings. Feeling a sense of urgency as the other climbers were quickly reaching Gene's perch on the wall, I motored up the crack, stuffing cams into the crack, and just gettin er done. I figured that, at least, we were destined for aid climbing in Yosemite later in the trip, and it would serve as practice, which it did and which I needed.

I clipped into an anchor and belayed Gene up. Just as he started up the pitch, the leading climber from the other party started up directly behind him. I had a feeling of dread that this would cause an argument between us, as the climber didn't give Gene much space. Gene quickly climbed up the pitch, blowing on his hands for warmth.

"It's a couple of Euros behind us," he said. "That guy is super strong. You see how he's floating up the crack."

I looked down and sure enough there he was, happily floating along where I just struggled. "This is hard…it is cold," the Swiss guy said in broken English.

We were impressed and didn't have any sort of conflict when he arrived at our belay. In fact, he was friendly and cheerful as could be. Gene set off on the next pitch, a hand crack through a small roof with face holds up a steep, green colored, lichen covered face. I sat shivering with the Swiss climbers as we joked in broken English about being cold. It was their first trip to the United States, and their first time on desert cracks. Geez, I thought, I've been climbing in the desert for a decade and these guys are already better than me on their first trip. But stronger climbers always have lessons to teach, and Gene and I both watched the duo in awe as they passed us after the next pitch.

After Gene's lead, I climbed through a small tunnel to a nice perch, which we would have enjoyed more if it weren't so damn cold. We laughed at how incorrectly described the pitch was on our topo, from an old Falcon guidebook, which made it sound runout and scary. The Swiss climbers happily and quickly climbed above, with inspiring, jealousy inducing efficiency up another splitter, mostly hands crack.

All of a sudden we heard a loud chopper noise piercing through the canyon, echoing off the many red rock walls that surrounded us. It was a helicopter, and it likely meant that a climber was hurt.

Helicopters are all too common in Red Rocks. Climbers are injured or killed every season, and the local police perform all rescues with helicopters. As Gene was midway up the next pitch the noise of the helicopter grew louder and louder and finally was a hundred feet behind us. All of this was distracting to him, as he just wanted to climb the pitch in peace and quiet. I watched in amazement as the helicopter landed on a small ledge hundreds of feet off the ground and parallel to us, dropping off a rescuer and then flying away. The rescuer, a police officer started yelling at us, "Are you okay?"

"Yes, we are," one of the Swiss climbers yelled back, and then generously added in an adorable accent, "Do you need our help?" Strong climbers and humanitarians!

The rescuer yelled back, "Do you know where Crimson Chrysalis is?"

All of this fuss continued to frustrate Gene. We both later agreed that the rescuers should know where one of the most, if not the most, popular route in the canyon was. The Swiss climbers finally yelled back directions, and the helicopter returned to pick the officer off the ledge. We continued the climb in the cold. The helicopter continued to circle the wall, finally reaching the injured climber.

We were bummed about the injury, which probably involved the couple that we had talked to just before. We never really found out exactly what happened, but it was a sobering event to start the trip with.

The injury and subsequent rescue was all too familiar to Gene, who had recently been in a climbing accident. It was the result of a fifty foot fall in the Black Canyon in Colorado the previous spring; a fall that could have killed him, but luckily only resulted in a broken hand. A man of incredible spirit, Gene fought heroically to get back in shape and eventually return to climbing. When he couldn't climb, he channeled his energy into epic runs in Telluride, running up multiple mountains in a session, putting in up to twenty miles per day.

The first thing we decided when we got off the Cloud Tower was that it was indeed too cold to comfortably climb in the shade this time of year. So the next day we would climb something that was south facing. We wanted to keep our good momentum going, so we decided to do another longer route the following day.

We celebrated with just the right amount of spirits and got to bed at a decent hour. We woke up again with the sun. Red Rocks always has these sublime sunrises, with an orange, red, pink fusion of color. Sometimes I think about the souls who have been up all night in Vegas; it's a feeling of pity, really, because I know the feeling of getting up early and doing physical activity is superior to the feeling of partying all night, and it's better for the soul.

All jazzed up on coffee, we drove the Freedom Mobile from camp over to Red Rocks. It's a shame, really, that one has to do this, because you can't camp inside Red Rocks, and then you have to pay an entrance fee every day that you enter the park.

So we paid the fee, parked the Freedom Mobile and then hiked up the trail into the canyon again. It's basically the same thing we did the day before, waking up early, hiking through a wash and then finding a big chunk of rock to climb.

We followed the wash up Oak Creek Canyon, almost to its end, for over an hour to the Eagle Wall. The wall was basking in the sun, and that was exactly what we were looking for, almost a thousand feet of vertical rock in front of us, all to ourselves. The only other people in sight were up on the wall on a different line, the classic and popular Levitation 29.

At the base of the dark, varnished wall we were assembling our rack together for the climb when we heard, "Rooooooock," and a softball sized chunk crashed to the ground from 300 feet above, next to our gear, barely missing us.

I wasn't surprised by the rock fall, the word was that Red Rocks just received an unusual amount of rain in the weeks prior, and we'd already heard multiple stories in the campground about broken holds.

We began up the wall. I led up a relatively easy crack, carefully placing gear in the cracks. The rock was wonderful, perfect edges that felt like they were designed for a human being to grip. On the second pitch the difficultly increased, but there were bolts to supplement the gear, very safe climbing. Pushing our way up the wall was joyful, and the temperature was perfect; we were basking in the sun, and most importantly getting a good workout in the vertical with ideal company.

After more and more delicate edging up the wall, we were at a perch where we could look out and see the Las Vegas Strip, which almost seemed small from the view we had; so different from driving in at night and seeing the light pollution from an hour away, then getting closer and closer and the light just dominates everything. The perspective in the vertical is always much different than the horizontal. The mighty walls of Red Rocks that nature made are much more impressive than the monuments of hotels and casinos.

With just the right amount of daylight left, we arrived at the last pitch, with about 800 feet of air below us. Looking at our topo from that old Falcon guide, it appeared to be a casual finish, only 5.9 and just eighty feet of climbing. I was perplexed when I heard Gene struggling up the groove.

"This is hard Luke, I don't know."

"You got it," I said, it's what I always say.

There is always a mental struggle when a climber is leading, to climb above one's gear, to take that risk of falling, of failure or, worse, getting injured. Knowing that Gene has recently hurt himself in a big fall, he's more prone to the voices of doubt inside his head, voices and fear that will now be harder to harness and quiet.

But Gene completed the section without falling, and I followed up. The climbing was different than the solid, dark brown, varnished rock we started on, up higher it is white and sandy and really difficult. I started to make some funny whimpering voices as well as I inched up on toprope, and when I finally reached Gene's belay I congratulated him on a job well done.

"That was some hard 5.9," I said and Gene agreed. Later, when we purchased an updated guide, we learned that the pitch was actually much harder and considered to be the most difficult crux pitch on the climb.

We rappelled down the face, and, of course, the rope got stuck in a crack. We had to climb back up to retrieve it, and by then the daylight was quickly fading. I took one more look back towards Vegas, and the sunset was quite similar to the sunrise, a set of colors that would soon be replaced with the lights of the night.

By the time we got off the wall, we had just a few minutes of light left, and then it all went away. We were a bit bummed because this meant there were more chances for getting lost on the descent, and that is exactly what happened. Instead of going down the way we approached the wall, I led us down a different slab, and then we entered a long chimney system, choked with trees and bushes, and just a generally unpleasant place to be.

By now, it was pitch dark, and we were down climbing a steep chimney system with our backpacks. At one point, the dirty chimney narrowed down so much I decided to throw my pack down; when I did it fell fifty more feet than I thought it would. I then realized my camera was in the pack, and my car keys, and was hoping I could even get to my pack, and if I couldn't, well, we're fucked.

But I climbed down to it, and everything was fine and Gene hucked his pack down the chimney too, and we climbed and climbed, down out of the gully, finally reaching the wash. The sandy wash was like a rabbit hole, on and on, until finally we were out of it and we hiked back to the Freedom Mobile to celebrate.

After three days of climbing we were ready to rest and sick of the fees that Red Rocks demands, so we figured we might as well go down to Joshua Tree, just four hours away, to celebrate Halloween. I lived in J-Tree for a winter and had always heard Halloween was a great time, so we decided to check it out.

We knew California was going to love the Freedom Mobile, and we felt at ease as it crossed over the border to the Golden State. Soon we were immersed in a desert of Joshua Trees on a lonesome highway, and I had a feeling of going home. I felt good too, because even if the Freedom Mobile were to break down, we could just tow it to the town of J-Tree, and we could still climb. I was always worrying about the Freedom Mobile breaking down, and Gene was always confident it wouldn't. What made me worry, other than the obvious, was that seven out of the nine warning lights had come on, on the dashboard. The check engine light was on for the first time in the Freedom Mobile's history, and the trunk light was on, because I'd ripped off the spoiler a few weeks before the trip. I'd ripped off the spoiler because I was afraid it would fall off, as the front bumper did a year before. But, alas, the Freedom Mobile rolled into J-Tree without incident.

It had been three years since I'd been to J-Tree, but things didn't seem to change much: still a dusty, rustic, small downtown, with the busy California highway rolling through it. Small town America, with much of the business aimed at the climbers and other tourists that pass through.

We stopped into the library for a quick check of the weather, as we promised each other that we would beeline it up to Yosemite if the weather improved. Sure enough, the online weather showed that it would be in the seventies in Yosemite in a couple days. The minute I showed Gene this there was an electric feeling; we would be going to Yosemite after the Halloween weekend in J-Tree.

J-Tree was crowded, as it was a Friday, and the start to a big weekend. We wanted a prime spot in the best campground, Hidden Valley, where we knew the Halloween party would be. Hidden Valley is also close to a hundred or so great rock climbs; so once the Freedom Mobile was there we would be all set up for our weekend.

Eventually we scored a spot in Hidden Valley. I was psyched to see several climbers already in costume for Halloween. Immediately, the Freedom Mobile was getting approval, with nods and thumbs up from fellow climbers who walked by our campsite.

We didn't do too much climbing; we were pretty worked from the three days in Red Rocks, so we took it easy on ourselves. Nothing can destroy the vibe of a good climbing trip worse than overdoing it. Climbing contains its magic with just the right amount of dosage. Plus, we were headed to Yosemite soon, and we had big goals for climbing there.

We just enjoyed the California sunshine and visiting with other climbers. Already, within half an hour of arriving at the site, we ran into two different groups of climbers that we knew. One friend, Holly, that I knew from my college days in Gunnison, hooked Gene up with some costume attire, most notably a curly blue wig that went down past his shoulders. I already had a costume box in the car, and lent Gene some items as well, rounding out his outfit. By Halloween, we were ready to properly celebrate.

I woke up and put on my costume: first the grey wig, then the one piece pink jump suit, and finally a black leather belt with metal loops that I could clip my chalk bag onto. Gene's costume was even more over the top: the curly blue wig with an American flag bandana tied across it, a vintage, late 1960s psychedelic shirt, and blue jeans.

We climbed a few pitches, in costume, attracting strange looks from some climbers and shouts of approval from others. Other climbers were in costume as well, a tradition that holds strong in J-Tree.

We did the classic Geronimo climb, in camp, a moderate but overhanging crack that splits a roof. Tradition demands that one climber climbs up to the top of the roof, locks his feet off in the crack and yells, "Geronimooooooooo," which echoes throughout the campsite below. I was climbing second, on top rope, and did the deed, hanging upside down in my pink one piece, careful to hold on to my wig so it did not fall off.

Rappelling down, Gene got his blue wig stuck in the rappelling device, which would have been a problem if it was his real hair; long haired and especially dreadlocked climbers have run into this potentially dangerous situation in the past.

After a couple roped pitches, we got rid of the gear, and just scrambled on the rocks around camp, ropeless, in costume, hooting and hollering when we reached the top. We stashed cans of beer in our pockets to drink on the top of the hundred foot domes, which looked over the landscape, all blue skies and Joshua trees and granite domes for as far as the eye could see. An occasional plane from the nearby military base would fly by, seeming out of place in the peaceful setting of Joshua Tree.

Scrambling down just as the sun was setting, there was a troop of people in costumes parading through camp, announcing what campsite was hosting the big party. It was a classic climber party with all kinds of fun people in a variety of costumes from mullet wigs to one piece wrestling outfits. An aluminum foil robot was cranking the tunes, and a big dance party ensued around the campfire.

At one point, a big portion of the party left for the Chasm of Doom, a big tunnel-chimney system that is a popular nighttime excursion during and after climber parties. I'd done it before and opted to not go. Gene, on the other hand, was psyched and disappeared off into the night with a crew of a dozen or so drunken climbers.

In the morning we woke up hungover. Gene was covered in scrapes and cuts that he acquired in the Chasm of Doom. He'd also lost one of his flip-flops, and the blue wig. I remembered why I chose not to go. We had our fun in Joshua Tree, and it was time to get serious about climbing again. We packed up the Freedom Mobile and headed up to Yosemite.

The Freedom Mobile still had the check engine light on, but it continued to float on down the highway, so we just kept rolling. It was a funky little highway out of Joshua Tree that led us to the interstate, one of those interstates where you can see the smog from miles away, and sense the gloom of it all.

It was this sort of highway that carried us to Yosemite, the big wall Mecca of the world. Gene and I bought two weeks of groceries, stuffing the Freedom Mobile to the brim with the type of supplies that one needs for big wall climbing: canned food, coffee, granola bars, and gas for the stove. We rolled into the park late, haggard from the road, and headed straight to the Green House.

The air was unexpectedly warm for November in Yosemite as we got out of the Freedom Mobile. We were pleased that we didn't have to sleep in Camp 4, the climber's campground that was once a pleasant place to camp back when Gene and I were still in our diapers. These days Camp 4 is a potentially grim place to stay for several reasons, mainly the park rangers, who highly regulate the typically crowded campsites, so much that one does not feel free or at ease while camping. Once, I was woken up in the middle of the night by a ranger asking for my camping permit.

The rustic Green House was more than welcoming. In the living room were Scott and Ned, our friends who lived in the house, and two of their friends, fellow climbers, destined to be our friends as well. We cracked beers and toasted to the possibility of good climbing weather in November.

Gene and I were set on climbing El Capitan, the largest rock face in the Lower 48. Neither of us had climbed it before, and we thought that this was the trip. In the morning, over coffee, we decided that we would start up the wall the following day.

Driving into the valley that morning we met up with our friend Mark, who works as a guide in Yosemite. He was finishing up his season as the Valley was slowing down with winter on its way. We mentioned that we were going to start up the Nose on El Capitan the following day, and he asked if he could join. Mark has made several trips up The Captain and he is a fun and energetic guy; we didn't mind at all if he joined. Immediately, we noticed that Mark's demeanor was erratic. First he could go, and then he could not. He was busy moving out of his place for the season, and seemed to have a lot on his mind. To make matters more complicated, Scott called and said he would like to join us as well.

That afternoon, while Scott was working and Mark was busy with errands, Gene and I went to the El Capitan meadow, just to stare at it, and see how many climbers were on the 3,000 foot wall. Incredibly, we could only see one solo climber, high on the Nose. It was a great feeling to know we would finally be climbing on El Capitan the following day; both of us had been making trips to Yosemite over the last ten years, and neither of us had climbed it. The first time I saw El Capitan it seemed so big, so improbable to want to climb it. Now, finally, after honing our skills for years and years it was time to try to climb The Big Stone. I was full of confidence and motivation. My recent climb of the Painted Wall in the Black Canyon had me convinced that I could now climb El Cap. After all, if I had the skills to get up the biggest cliff in Colorado, I could get up the tallest one in California, right?

"Gene, maybe after we climb the Nose we could do the Salathe Wall. It would be really cool to climb it twice don't you think?" I said.

Gene mumbled something at the ridiculous ambition of my comment, and we continued to tilt our necks back looking up at over 3,000 feet of sheer, golden granite.

We went back to the Green House to pack up for the climb. It was frantic. I wasn't happy that we were, all of a sudden, a team of four. But, plans kept changing throughout the day, so I knew there was a chance that something would happen and things would change again.

We laid out a tarp and stuffed two big haul bags, nearly the size of a man, and almost the weight of one. Mark continued to be frantic, "So there is a chance I have to work, if so, I'll just rappel off with an extra rope."

Mark's demeanor didn't get me psyched, and I made subtle hints about how a team of four might be too much. We were hungry for the big wall experience, and Mark was clearly low on excitement for the experience. He'd been living and working in Yosemite for almost six months and didn't have the fire. I was beginning to think he just wanted to hang out with us, and this was how he was going about it.

Mark is one of my best friends, no Mark is like a brother, a soul mate that shares the love of climbing, so I just put my head down and continued to pack up. Scott finally showed up and confirmed that he was in. He laid out his gear on the gigantic tarps and started stuffing it in.

By this time it was dark and we had moved inside the Green House and were still packing. In addition to this, we were drinking and smoking and getting weary. Scott's roommate Ned, a big wall veteran himself, just looked at us and could sense the madness and the confusion.

Finally, near the end of the packing, Mark quickly reached into the haulbag to find something, accidentally pulled out a carabiner, which smacked him in the face, knocking out half of one of his front teeth. Suddenly it was quiet. Scott whispered what we were all thinking, that Mark would not be coming up the wall. He would have to visit a dentist in the morning. He was bummed but stayed in good spirits. Mark started removing his gear from the bags. Late in the night I crawled in to my tent for a few hours of sleep. I set my alarm for 4:20 a.m.

The alarm went off and I felt tired. Like a true fiend, I headed straight inside to get coffee going. The coffee ignited the fire of my determination to finally climb El Capitan, and I felt motivated. Gene made up some grub, and we packed the two large haul bags into the Freedom Mobile.

It was still dark as we drove from Foresta into the Valley. We parked the Freedom Mobile by the El Cap meadow, and made the short approach to the wall. After the coffee wore off I felt tired, and the task of humping our gear to El Cap, while short, was draining. I looked at Gene, with the haulbag on his back, and he was sweating heavily. Scott, on the other hand, seemed to be in his element, accepting all of these struggles as part of the game.

Since Scott was the aid climbing expert, it was agreed he would lead the first block of pitches. He started up, moving quickly, and then commenced the hauling of the pigs (the haul bags). They didn't budge on the slab and Gene had to push them up to get started. At that moment, Gene and I knew we were in for some serious suffering and hard work, and we looked at each other.

I said, "You know we probably should have done a practice aid wall before jumping on El Cap." He looked back and agreed, with the ocean of golden granite towering above us.

Finally, Gene had to jumar up to assist Scott with the hauling, as they both grunted and struggled to move the haul bags inches. I jumared up as well and thought about the time that had passed since we'd started the pitch. When we reached the second pitch, well over two hours had passed, and I thought of how daring, expert, big wall Yosemite climbers had speed climbed the entire route in the time it took us to get up the first two hundred feet.

The suffering and turmoil got worse as the morning progressed and turned into the afternoon. There were traversing pitches where I had to lower out the two haul bags so that Scott and Gene could haul. I'd never done this, and the weight of the bags pulled terrifyingly on me. I was to the point of cursing and complaining already. But, a party was behind us, and a woman was leading up behind me, and there was no way I was about to have a meltdown in front of another climber, a female one at that, just a few pitches up on El Cap.

The woman arrived at my belay as I struggled with the haul bags, and she clipped into the same bolted anchor I was using. She and her partner were only doing the initial pitches of the climb, and so were equipped with a light, free climbing rack and nothing else, the same style that the speed climbing aces use to run up the wall in a few hours.

They looked so free and happy. I was having problems un-weighting the haul bag from the anchor, and the woman helped me get the weight of the bags off the anchor by pushing up on them, so they could be lowered out with the remaining rope. "How far are you all going today?" she asked.

"Uh, I think we need to go back to the drawing board, maybe go do a shorter aid route," I replied. I was already coming to the realization that Gene and I had a lot to learn about big wall aid climbing before trying to climb El Cap.

At this ledge I thought about style, and hated that we had so much weight and it was such a task to haul all the supplies up. I thought about how we had come all the way out to Yosemite just to suffer like this, because, after all, even if we did not realize it at the time, we were doing exactly what we'd come to do. To learn to big wall aid climb is to suffer, and then, after that suffering, the knowledge is attained and the rewards are found.

Finally, Scott and Gene began the hauling and I started up the pitch. There was a traversing section where I had to lower myself out with the extra rope that was dangling off my harness. I'd never done this before and was terrified. Scott, just forty feet above, was close enough that he could offer a tutorial of how it was done. I finally lowered myself out, and like many climbing procedures, it was not as scary as the initial perception in my head. We were lucky to have Scott on board, and if Mark were there he could have provided beneficial lessons as well. Gene and I had a lot to learn.

When I arrived at the belay with Scott and Gene we had an enormous eruption of laughter at our struggle. I couldn't recall the last time I laughed that hard, and felt a weight off my shoulders as I laughed to the point of tears.

We were at a spot where we could rappel down directly in a short amount of time, so we debated what we were going to do. Scott was game to continue, and I think Gene could have gone either way. I'd made my mind up at the last belay that I wanted to hone my skills some more before climbing The Captain. I expressed this to my friends, and they obliged to retreat. Sometimes admitting failure can be a blow to a climber's ego, but, at that point, I had no ego to be had. I imagined I was the worst aid climber in Yosemite, and didn't give a damn, which, in itself, was a relief and a revelation. Freedom is just another word for nuthin' left to lose, right?

Retreat was not as easy as we imagined. At that point there were now five climbers at the belay ledge, us and the other party. There wasn't any tension though, which can happen at a crowded belay ledge, especially with failure in the air. We were sitting there trying to figure out how to rappel off with the mighty haul bags the weight of a man. The woman's partner, a big wall veteran himself, originally from Alabama, who'd already been up El Capitan, and all the other walls in Yosemite, advised us to simply lower the bags off as one of us rappelled down and clipped the bag into the next anchor. He was right, it was the most efficient way to do it, rather than having one of us rappel with the bags attached to us, and fumble down the wall. He was hilarious too, as we messed with the bags.

At one point Scott had the bags in between his legs, and he joked, "I bet you always wanted to ride a fat chick huh?" in a way that only a Southerner could say.

We talked to him more as Scott rappelled down, "Oh man you guys are trying El Cap for your first big wall in Yosemite? That's ambitious. I did five or six practice walls before getting on this thing. Almost died once of heatstroke on the Leaning Tower, trying to climb it in the summer, we were so stupid..." he went on with his stories. Big wall climbers all have these stories, and more proof in my mind that every wall climber suffers for every bit of glory attained.

I was feeling glorious and relieved when we finally touched back on the ground. It wasn't the goal, the goal was to top out on El Cap, three or so days later, but I'd learned some valuable lessons. Gene and I talked it over, and we would take a rest day, repack and then attempt a shorter big wall route.

The weather was still sunny and warm, blue skies and all, a blessing for early November. Mark wanted to do some sport climbing, so we met up with him in the early afternoon the next day. Sport climbing is somewhat of a rarity for Yosemite, traditional in its nature.

We hiked up to some obscure wall for a couple routes. The trees were changing colors, the gigantic Yosemite Falls still had some water flowing down it, and we even had a bear leisurely stroll by in the forest below us.

Mark was loving it. He was over the suffering of big walls and just wanted to bask in the simple play that is sport climbing. He made us laugh as he jokingly used his new kneepads that he was going to use for overhanging sport climbing in Mexico, where he lives and works in the winter with his girlfriend.

That night we packed up the haulbag, one haulbag, because it was just going to be Gene and me for the climb. We decided to go for the all time beginner's classic, the South Face of the Washington Column, a thousand plus foot wall of mostly straightforward aid climbing. Gene and I both had failed previously on this route, so there was also the prospect of redemption, something that always sweetens the deal when figuring out what to climb. I'd also done the classic free climb, Astroman, on the same wall, with Mark the previous summer, in nine hours, which gave me confidence that we could get up the South Face in two days, even with all the extra baggage for living and sleeping on the wall.

There was an air of calm as we packed up the bag in the Green House. Ned and Scott watched us pack. Scott talked of plans to do a nearby climb to ours, Southern Man, with another climbing partner on our second day, so it would be a party on the wall. We continued to pack and organize late in the night, and Ned stayed up with us, saying he wanted to be part of the excitement. He commented that he could sense we were going to be successful this time, and I took that to be a blessing and a good sign.

We woke up around 4:20 again, completed the ritual of coffee, eating, and pooping, and made our way into The Valley in the dark. Funny thing about climbing the Washington Column, one parks his car in the parking lot for the upscale Ahwahnee hotel; it's an atrocity if you ask me, that there is a luxurious hotel in a National Park dedicated to preserving a natural environment. I say tear it down, and build more campsites and housing for the park employees, who for the most part live in small, uncomfortable quarters. Regardless, it felt strange as we parked the Freedom Mobile next to all the nice BMWs, Hummers, and other vehicles for rich folk, pulled the haulbag out of the car and started hiking up to the wall.

As we were getting our gear together we noticed another duo doing exactly what we were doing. Since the South Face is so popular we figured they were getting on the same route we were. We weren't exactly psyched on the prospect of getting stuck behind another party so we tried to get our act together and started hiking to the wall. I led us astray at one point, hiking past the trailhead that heads up to the Washington Column, but luckily we got to the base of the route just before the other party, again, possibility for tension as they arrived just five minutes after we had. The first thing they said was, "I hope you boys are ready to party on the ledge. We got some whiskey," and both Gene and I were relieved they weren't going to be impatient with us.

The South Face of the Washington Column is a genius route to get acclimated on the rituals and mechanisms of big wall climbing, provided it's not a traffic jam with too many climbers. One can climb the wall with only hauling the bag for three pitches up to Dinner Ledge, leaving them there after spending the night on the ledge, climbing to the top of the wall, and then rappelling back to the bag, much lighter after two days, and finally rappelling with the bag back to the ground.

We fought and struggled with the haul bag for three pitches, maybe four hundred feet or so, cursing and sweating, till we finally reached Dinner Ledge, a urine smelling, but glorious place to be. We basically collapsed on the ledge for a while, laying out our sleeping territory, taking our stove and food out of the haul bag and all the other little comforts we had to set ourselves up to enjoy a night on the wall.

Our new friends, Ben and Patrick, progressed below us at about the same pace we did, and we exchanged friendly remarks to one another as they came up to the ledge. They were able to find their own little perch to sleep on, just five feet higher and thirty or so feet adjacent to our own little camp.

After resting for a bit, we did another couple pitches. I led, as we were doing the climbing in blocks, and on the second pitch I started to feel comfortable in the environment. I'd been here before. Half Dome, to the east, stood proudly, looking over us and seeming to give us its blessing. The aid climbing movement, stepping in our ladder-like sling aiders, much different than the progress of free climbing, using only one's hands and feet, finally felt right and efficient. On the last pitch of the day, I was finally feeling a flow on the golden granite wall. I moved quickly, and Gene made positive remarks about my progress, which made me feel good. There was a small, easy pendulum, which I completed, gently swinging over, and I felt like a child lost in play. I clipped into the anchors and set the ropes up for Gene, while Half Dome sat there in the shade, trickling waterfalls loomed in the distance and birds circled us.

When Gene reached my point of the pendulum, he would have to do a lower-out, as I did on El Cap. I walked him through it, trying to remember how it went. He looked as I must have felt two days ago, fumbling with the ropes, convincing himself that he was doing the right thing.

"Are you sure, this is how it goes?" he said. "I think so, yes, I mean it is."

He finally figured it out, and we rappelled down to the ledge, leaving the rope fixed so that we could jumar up it in the morning.

We got comfortable on our bivy ledge, and it was one of the most glorious evenings of my life. I'd stayed at this ledge once previously on a failed attempt of the route, and that night I never quite felt calm and at ease. For whatever reason this night was different. We stared at Half Dome, as it finally got some of the days last rays of sun: gray granite with black water streaks and hints of orange. I had the feeling I was exactly where I was supposed to be. Gene and I were proud, and we were on the heels of success. All we had above us was climbing, and we didn't have to worry about the pains of hauling.

The simple Indian food out of a Tasty Bites package tasted like the best meal of my life. The one and a half beers we had were savored in small sips. (We lost half of one beer as the can had punctured, slowly leaking out in to the haulbag.) We had two small speakers and a tiny iPod, and the music gently serenaded us with the high vibes and spirits of the vertical world.

I thought of the past, I thought of the climber who was killed on this very same ledge, by rockfall dislodged from another party high up on the route, on pitches not recommended to do by the guide because another party is almost always below you on this route. I thought of his partner, and his family, and how the incident affected them. Across from us on the 2,000-plus foot granite slab named Glacier Point, a young climber named Peter Terbush, from Gunnison, had been killed by rockfall. So much reminder of death, yet we felt safe, peaceful, content, alive, so psyched. I wondered what happened to their spirits, where they existed now?

I thought of my last bivy, unplanned and without sleeping gear on the Painted Wall, in the Black Canyon, a sleepless night huddled next to my companion, shivering, just waiting for the endless night to be over. Perhaps that was why this bivy felt so good, so right, remembering the one that was full of dread and cold.

I thought of Layton Kor, the prolific climber of the 1960s who had established this route, as well as the Black Canyon route I suffered on in the unplanned bivy. I read in the guidebook that he and his partner, Chris Fredericks, didn't get to stay on this ledge and rather pressed on for higher terrain eventually spending a sleepless night hanging in slings. I thought about how drive and passion for climbing can sometimes make one overlook the gentler, simpler fruits of life.

Most of all I thought how lucky I was to be up there with Gene. We were in synch, and comfortable with one another in the vertical. He wanted this as badly as I did, and we were getting along famously. The boys came down and partied with us, as they promised. They were high on the vertical world too, and we made obscene jokes as guys do without women around, and laughed as if we were old friends. Finally it was time to sleep and we drifted off with the cosmos. I was warm in my sleeping bag, and could only fall to sleep after I tied in with the rope.

We woke up with the rays of the sun, forced down oatmeal and coffee, and pooped as one poops on a wall, first into a plastic bag, then stuffing the bag into the three foot long PVC pipe, called a poop tube. Immediately Gene started jumaring up the rope we'd fixed the previous afternoon, and I followed right up after him. Finally, I had a flow to my jumar techniques, and really felt good about how efficiently I was moving. We wanted to move quickly that day, both because success would be a big boost for our spirits, and because we wanted our new friends to be successful as well.

As Gene started leading up a small, thin crack we heard voices below, and it was Scott, with one of his friends climbing up to the Thanksgiving ledge. They were planning on a day climb of Southern Man, a harder route, within spitting distance of ours. It was incredible to watch their pace as I split my time keeping an eye on Gene as he led, and peering down as they raced up the wall. Gene fiddled above with nuts and cams, sliding them into the crack, as Scott did the same. They quickly reached our level, close enough that we could talk as I picked Scott's brain about aid climbing questions, and we made obscene jokes and shouted loudly and just generally hooted and hollered, buzzed on life in the vertical.

Clouds began forming, some grayness looming in the background, but no thunder or lightning. We had a good chance to get up this wall.

Scott's big wall climbing technique and demeanor is unique. He was talking to himself, singing a version of some reggae, and yelling at his partner the whole time, inching tiny stoppers and cam hooks in the cracks. "Oh God, this is sketchy," he said, all while having a smile on his face. A master at work.

Gene kept leading as I followed and cleaned. Our new friends below were progressing nicely, and all was well on the wall. Once they reached the belay where I was it would usually be time for me to set off and clean the pitch. Finally, we finished the aid climbing section, and it

73

was time for a few pitches of free climbing, our element. We ditched a bag with the aid climbing equipment at a belay, and I set off leading. The clouds were getting worse, and the wind was picking up. I tried to climb as fast as possible, while not trying to climb too fast and make a silly mistake, like a fall, that would slow us down. As I climbed I felt so determined to get up the thing; this climb would define our trip.

At the second to last pitch, there was a point where there was an intimidating, off-width-squeeze chimney above, the one Layton Kor had surely led on the first ascent. To the right was another option, an ugly awkward seam that had been hammered with pitons. In our home multi-pitch area, the Black Canyon, that would have been unacceptable to hammer an easier option just fifteen feet over from the true, proud line. But, every area has its own practices, and I opted for the quicker mode of climbing, the easier, quicker seam. I did make a mental note, to return to take the more proud line. A great thing about climbing, those rocks will always be there.

Gene led the last pitch, with a funky, fun move over a small roof, and I followed up. We'd climbed the route. We shook hands, and it was anticlimactic, of course. Clouds and winds increased, and we knew we just had to get off this damn thing, and we rigged a rappel. The wind blew our ropes all over the place, and rappelling was a mixture of prayers and experience, just hoping they would not get stuck, which could cause all types of problems.

We rappelled past Ben as he was leading up. He was struggling in a chimney section, and I remembered how he said the night before that he hated chimneys. I kept rappelling and noticed an anchor just to the right of where Patrick was belaying from, but didn't give much of a thought to its purpose and clipped into the bolts at Patrick's belay. Gene did the same, and we pulled the rope, hoping not to hit Ben. It was a bit of a clusterfuck. As we pulled the rope it got stuck, we tugged some more and it was indeed not going anywhere. We frantically yelled to Ben, "Can you see where it's stuck."

"Let me see what I can do," Ben said. "Oh, shit I can't move."

Our rope had wrapped around him and his gear, and he could not climb up. He had to rappel down. We felt so bad. Patrick had finally lost most of his patience with us, but was still polite. What a guy! They wanted redemption and success on this wall, just as we did. Ben finally fixed everything, and as he did so, I realized the adjacent set of anchors were for rappelling, and set where they were so that the rope would not get stuck in the chimney above. Another lesson learned, but at the expense of our new friends, damn. I wondered if we would have had the same patience with them if the roles had been reversed.

We kept rappelling and the winds kept getting more and more intense as we came down. When we tossed the ropes they went completely sideways, horizontal, and we just prayed they would not get stuck. Luckily they didn't. We finally reached the Dinner Ledge, gathering up our gear, and quickly headed down three more rappels, finally reaching the ground. Success! But, I couldn't help but feel bad as we looked up at the wall as Ben and Patrick were rappelling down. We could see their headlamps. Not only did they not reach the top, but also they had to rappel in the wind, in the dark.

We made it back to the Freedom Mobile, never hard to find in a parking lot, especially one with nice, shiny cars. We bee-lined it straight to the grocery store and bought beers to celebrate, meeting Scott back at the Green House for a humble dinner of pasta.

It stormed that night, and I slept in my tent to the sound of rain. Higher up it had snowed. As we were making breakfast we heard a knock on the door. It was a Scottish couple. They'd had an epic journey the night before trying to drive into The Valley. They were following the GPS from their rental vehicle that had led them down a seldom used 4x4 road. By the time they realized they needed to turn around they were well down the road, and then got stuck and had to spend the night sleeping in the vehicle. I wasn't surprised. In Foresta, it seems at least a car a day ends up in the area, as the GPS programming is wired wrong for the region. We were happy to help and warmed them up with eggs and coffee, as we sat by the fireplace.

Eventually, we drove them into The Valley in the Freedom Mobile, dropping them off at the mechanic. I'd anticipated possibly needing the help of others during this trip, so we were more than happy to lend a helping hand, building up karma points in case we needed help at some point. This was not the first we'd helped others on the trip: we'd already jumped two vehicles with the jumper cables Gene had wisely thrown in the back. For some reason people knew they could reach out to the Freedom Mobile for help.

The rest of our time in Yosemite was a wash. It just kept raining and snowing, a sign to move on. Plus time was winding down. I'd found a place to live in Durango, house sitting for a generous, retired couple who wanted to meet me before they took off to Mexico for the winter.

We spent a couple days chillin' at the Green House, drinking beer like we would be forever young. It did clear up the day we were leaving, and we were able to get a couple last pitches at the Cookie Cliff, some of the best, shorter crack climbs in Yosemite.

On our warm up, Gene led, but had some difficulties near the top of the pitch. He had done the climb easily before on previous trips, and was frustrated with himself and cursed. I'd noticed Gene had more mental struggles than before his accident, but at the same time he was climbing so hard and well it was easy to forget he'd just severely broken his hand. The scars were obviously not simply on his hand; his headspace had been affected too. When he got down I could sense his frustration, and we had a quiet moment. It didn't last long though; we decided to do one more climb and then make our way back home.

I lead the last pitch for Yosemite: it was a nice finger and hand crack in a dihedral that made me want to linger and climb more. But, we had to go. Our spirits were back up after that pitch, and we hopped in the Freedom Mobile to leave Yosemite, grateful for our experiences, and hungry for more. We promised each other that we would return someday to climb El Capitan together.

We decided to break the trip up, as the Freedom Mobile would not be happy with an eighteen hour drive back to Colorado. So we headed back to Las Vegas, where we would climb for a couple more days, then make the last leg of the trip back home.

We drove that day into the night on a binge of caffeine and junk food, through the endless interstate of California, finally to the bright lights of Vegas. Weary, we set up camp where we'd begun the great trip. I was haggard, but grateful the Freedom Mobile had started half of the journey back home.

In the morning, we met up with my old friend Brent, who had been living in Vegas, and working as a rigger for musical acts and other entertainment acts. I'd met Brent in my college days in Gunnison and always looked up to him as a climbing hero. He was a big wall veteran, with everything from nine day winter solo ascents in the Black Canyon to scary, big wall aid climbs on El Capitan under his belt.

He'd moved to Vegas on a whim many years ago with the prospect of rigging work, and told us his life story of recent times. He'd married and been all over the country with work. I hadn't seen him in six years, since he'd given a slideshow at the college in Gunnison, after an epic alpine climb in Chamonix, France, with the legendary and late Jonny Copp, where Brent had lost most of his toes to frostbite.

Brent took us to Calico Basin, a bouldering area we'd never been to, and we were delighted because we didn't have to pay an entrance fee. I was wondering if Brent still had the drive for climbing after all he'd been through, and found out right away that he did, after warming up on a twenty five foot highball boulder problem.

Gene followed, so I had to as well. It was a great bouldering session, and Gene came alive. I think he wanted some redemption after his last lead in Yosemite. Brent's climbing inspired both of us, given that he barely had any toes, and was still climbing hard. At one point Gene found himself fifteen feet up a boulder, with another twelve to go, that point where falling isn't really an option, and success depends on focus and gentle climbing. He was up there for a while. I would have been worried but Gene seemed in control, calm, in meditation. He was sorting out things in his mind, and finished the climb with precision. Brent and I watched in awe, as he collectedly completed the sequence. Gene was searching for that mental state we all need in climbing, that peaceful calm in the face of danger. He was getting it back. The climb was so tall and difficult that neither Brent nor I dared repeat Gene's boldness.

We cranked a bit too hard on that bouldering session, given that our bodies were dehydrated after the long drive from Yosemite, and we woke up that next morning with hurting tendons. We decided to take the day for errands and put some new tires on the Freedom Mobile. The guys at the tire place joked about the car, "If I had a car like that, I'd be screwing girls that were named Moonbeam." They were missing the point, but we didn't care, they seemed harmless with their jokes so we laughed along.

Eventually, it was time for the last push back to Colorado. I felt drained. We'd been drinking beer, and eating just bread and pasta. On the drive, I felt an overwhelming need for the healing comforts of life. I longed for the soft touch of a woman, for a bed, a shower, for vegetables. Strung out from the road, and worked from three weeks of climbing.

Our luck continued and so did the enthusiasm from random people on the highway. Just entering Utah, an old woman with oxygen hooked up to her nose, sitting in the passenger seat of a truck looked over at us and smiling ear to ear at the sight of the Freedom Mobile, gave us a big thumbs up. At another gas station in the middle of nowhere, Utah, a group of mechanics smiled and said, "That looks like something Evil Knievel would drive." We were psyched on that one.

Gene took over the helm of the Freedom Mobile for the last stretch as I sat shotgun. I hadn't spent much time in the passenger seat of the vehicle, and eyed some features I'd never seen before. Looking toward the steering wheel, I noticed a small tray, similar to the ashtray that I used for coins. I opened it, and to my surprise there were two silver dollars, one from 1978, the year I was born. Incredible! Gene and I laughed at our luck, and fortune, as we finally saw that wonderful Colorful Colorado sign and the Freedom Mobile had made it home.

All went well with meeting the couple whose house I'm now living in as I write this. They still let me stay in their nice, plush home, even after seeing the Freedom Mobile. "It looks like it's been through a war," the woman remarked upon seeing it.

I'm trying to keep the Freedom Mobile near Durango; if it should break down it would be nice to have it close, and not somewhere far, far from home. It's closing in on 220,000 miles, still losing some fluids, but, otherwise, purring like a kitten. Durango has some other spray painted art cars, and it fits in nicely here.

The leap of faith turned out well. Durango is a great winter climbing locale. The granite of El Capitan is still in my dreams, but it does not consume me. Someday, the time will be right. I've been eating more vegetables and drinking less. I still depend on the Freedom Mobile daily for the seven mile commute into town. It might break down someday, but I'm hoping it will make it to 300,000 miles, why not dream big right? In the times we're in right now, people seem to appreciate the Freedom Mobile, and I need it because I can't afford a new car.

If it does break down, somewhere along the road, hopefully close to home, I'll do my best to sit back, to transport my mind back in time, back to a trip I never thought could happen in such a vehicle, with a climbing partner who believed in freedom and the risks necessary to live with it.

This piece was originally published in The Climbing Zine, Volume 3.

11 ODE TO THE TOWNIE

Once they are awakened from winter hibernation, the townies rule Crested Butte. In no other place on God's green earth are they respected more than there. Watch how they command traffic: a seasoned CB driver will slow down from their already crawling pace to let one cross the street, waving the townie on to its destination. Its as if the normal rules of our industrial society were flipped upside down. Human powered transportation is given priority. Nearly everyone has one, some use their townies more often than their cars. Certainly, within town limits, Crested Butte is better experienced at the slow pace of the townie.

Some are a bit flashy; others are equal parts art and mode of transportation. The best townie will stop someone dead in their tracks to just admire its uniqueness and beauty. Some townies barely function for more than the few blocks they are needed. Rarely locked, even in front of a bar, which increases the chances it might be stolen, which happens occasionally, followed by a plea in the newspaper to be returned. And, they are even often returned, found discarded in someone's yard who may know the owner, or read the plea in the paper and recognized it. This is a connected community, and the townie is one connection we all share.

Like many who are a part of this community, I don't actually live in Crested Butte. I used to, but, even when I did, CB was basecamp to bigger adventures, to the backyard, the rocks and the trails. A couple years ago, my last summer living in CB, I saw the townie in a different light, that of the night.

With some friends, we'd signed up for the 24 hour Bridges of the Butte endurance townie extravaganza. This was an extreme idea: see how many laps around Crested Butte you could do in the hours of a single day. Our warm up was the Chainless Race that took place earlier in the week, an equally insane event involving a couple hundred costumed freaks, starting at the top of Kebler Pass and descending seven miles into town without a single stroke of a pedal. Physically it might have turned out to not be much of a warm up, but metaphysically it was.

Our team was the Chihuahua Chasers, named after a harrowing incident where we chased a tiny dog around the town of Gunnison for several hours as it cheated death by running across the highway and nearly every major intersection of town. We draped ourselves in costumes and assembled several townies that we hoped could last for several laps around town.

The daytime laps were fun, being cheered on by bystanders, fueling our stoke for this ridiculous test of stamina. The nighttime laps were unforgettable, bikes lit up like spaceships, not recalling what lap we were on, and not caring because what mattered was our presence on the townies, and the stars looking on in approval.

Our team traded townies, and my personal favorite was a lowrider, borrowed from a friend of a friend, mine for the moment; smooth flowing, sitting comfortably in the saddle, I felt like a kid lost in play, enjoying the simple pleasure of riding a bike for what it is, one of man's finest inventions. Surrounded by my friends, cruising together, we were like a bike gang, and we were all gangsters of love.

On the east side of the course, where there were no houses, and the town turns into dirt roads heading to the mountain, another crew had stopped. Decked in a hundred lights, with townies of all variations, they had obviously spent some time preparing for this moment. A small stereo played tunes that softly serenaded us more into the moment. The stars winked. It was a classic moment, very out of this world, but very Crested Butte. No words needed to be exchanged; we just soaked it in, and then pedaled some more, in our own little townie heaven.

This piece was originally published in the Crested Butte Magazine, Summer 2013.

12 MY FIRST PIECE FOR DURANGO

"Treat my last like my first and my first like my last
The song that I sing to you is my everything"

My First Song by Jay Z

It was the cold of Gunnison that sent him down south to
Durango. Cold in different ways: the temperature and the cold of heart.
One too many times did he have his heart broken, and he broke one
too many hearts.

He is without a past in Durango. He can walk the streets alone and
be almost certain that he won't be recognized. This won't last long, so
he takes it for what it is worth. He can sense the strong community by
how people interact, in the supermarket, the post office and
downtown. Durango in December, this year it has been warm,
pleasant, the high temperature of the day rising up to fifty degrees; a
pleasure to walk out into the afternoon Colorado sun, a blessing for the
heart and soul of a rock climber.

Naturally, he seeks out the climbing areas. Durango is like
Gunnison at first, no epic cliffs in sight when one rolls into town. A
little research and one finds there are cliffs all over: sandstone,
limestone and granite.

The traditional area of East Animas has gotten his attention. The
area's proudest crag, the Watch Crystal is almost two hundred feet, a
rainbow of sandstone. The view from the crag is expansive, farmland
just below, acres of it. Snowcapped mountains to the west, the La
Platas, begging for more snow, but the days lately have been all
sunshine, the blue bird sky that Colorado is famous for, an intoxicating
sunshine.

More cliffs off in the distance, multiple areas, they stand as
monuments to him that he is where he should be in life, with new cliffs
for him to explore, to climb, to grow older with. He has a few friends
to go climbing with, old Gunnison friends that now live in Durango, or
nearby. A blessing to have a comfort like that in a new town, people

---

that he knows to trust his life with on the other end of the rope. He needs the climbing; climbing is who he is, where he found courage and adventure and the need to be free, that need to breathe clean air and camp out in the dirt.

Climbing at East Animas is like anywhere else, with its own funkiness for added flavor and excitement. It demands one works for the gear that he places, hanging on by your fingers trying to wiggle a piece of gear in the crack, and then trying to worm up the route with some grace. He aims to make deliberate movements, as if he knows where he is going, but he has never been there. He's already been humbled here on moderate terrain, even to the point of embarrassment, but he loves climbing and he knows love is a powerful force that can endure.

The climbing is less crowded than he expected. It's so close to town, yet he only sees a handful of souls each day at the crags. But, maybe it's because it's December and the local climbers have switched to climbing ice or skiing. He'll find out in the spring. He sees the skiers drive by with their equipment strapped to the top of their vehicles, on their way up to Purgatory and Silverton, as he crosses the highway to another area, the Golf Wall. This wall, in the winter, feels like discovering a treasure; it just sits basking in the sun and warms up nicely. Even at a mere 32 degrees, with the sun, it is enjoyable, pure heaven. The climbing is overhanging limestone, sure to work the climber to failure, but failure and enduring is all part of the path, and again this is where the love comes in.

Just as he needs climbing to be who he truly is, he needs the love of a woman. Finding love is not as simple as finding the climbing areas. He's learned much about patience from climbing, and more than he wanted to about patience from love. Walking the streets of Durango, there is an abundance of beautiful women. With their presence they quiet his fears about loneliness; it is only a matter of time before he will connect with one of these beauties.

The scene is set for love to take place here, the warmth, the opportunity to hike into the mountains, to soak in hot springs; Durango has all the elements for romance to ensue. A slow turning novel it is, beautiful and demanding of patience. He should savor every day, every sentence, every word and every woman who strolls by. The prime of his life as a lover and climber is unfolding.

Slowly, the days will progress, and he will become more a part of the town. He will build a name for himself, and meet more and more people. As time goes by a woman will become the main character in the novel that is his life. That time to find her, though almost inevitable, seems like an eternity, like the time that it took Mother Nature to build the rocks he climbs upon in the afternoon sun.

He has survived eternity before, and he will again. He has loved before and will again. Climbing keeps his head on straight, his meditation that keeps the flesh patient. An activity that is a constant reminder to appreciate the day, the moment, all we really ever have as human beings. He knows he is just reading the first page of the place that is called Durango.

This piece was originally published in The Climbing Zine, Volume 3.

13 MEXICO BOUND, AIRPORT REFLECTIONS

On the flight out of Durango
An old woman tells me her story
Kids, husband, a military family

I tell her a little about my girlfriend
She asks, when are you getting married?
People want you to follow their path

An unexpected landing in another place other than my destination
Finally, we arrive in Denver, my plane to Mexico long gone
Tickets rebooked, time to chill, kill

Snow falls in April
It's always winter somewhere in Colorado
A young black man pushes an old white woman in a wheelchair
People get their shoes shined
Who owns shoes that need to be shined?

The New Belgium Brewery restaurant is a haven for lunch
A brief intoxication of one beer
I don't crave any more
I eat really bad Chinese food for dinner
And my soul feels empty

I dream of the woman I've been loving lately
I people watch and think how did we kill time
Without these glowing rectangles?
I watch TV shows, movies and read newspaper headlines
Here today, gone tomorrow

The most fascinating sight of all
A kid's basketball team in wheelchairs
One kid has only one full arm, no legs
They are smiling tossing two basketballs
Between the eight of them

They are smiling more than any of the other travellers I've seen
So much of life is perspective

The next plane is here
It will take me to Houston
I'll sleep terribly tonight
I hate sleeping in airports

But the sweet reward:
Climbing tomorrow in a Mexican limestone paradise
Then on Saturday a wedding of two people who love one another
And friends who love one another, and more new friends to meet
The flight in the sky leads somewhere
And then I'll do this all over again
I'll forget it all, the headlines, the random faces
But I'll never forget those kids
And what they showed me

14 THE FINE LINE BETWEEN TOURIST AND TRAVELLER

A while back, I read an article in the *Durango Herald* about an alliance created between the three Durangos: our beloved city, Spain and Mexico. From the tone of the piece it sounded like the communication has gone by the wayside, but it got me thinking of my own connection to our neighbors down south.

My travels to Latin America began with a three week trip to Costa Rica and Nicaragua before the start of my senior year of college in Gunnison. We volunteered, surfed, partied and rambled, seeing the lush, tropical countryside and returned with a changed view of the world, and a new appreciation for some of the simple luxuries we have as Middle Class Americans. I also realized I'd probably never make another international trip that didn't involved rock climbing.

A couple years later, a January trip was planned to El Potrero Chico, Mexico, a climbing area located just a few hours south of Laredo, Texas. When we were alerted to a travel advisory warning in Nuevo Laredo, Mexico, we almost bailed, but we ended up making the journey. What a revelation: only a day's drive from Colorado was a dangerous, almost lawless land, with endless limestone and prices just right for a dirtbag.

One climbing partner was scared of spiders, the other of snakes, and I was scared of everything. Their fears could have made for some good practical jokes, but nothing could have topped the real life situation, when my *amigo* who was deathly afraid of spiders hiked for an hour with a tarantula in his shoe, nestled under his arch. The whole hike he complained about his shoe feeling weird, and when he finally took it off he discovered the tarantula, screaming and sending an aftershock of terror so loud they could hear it up north in *Estados Unidos*.

When we reached the border town of Nuevo Laredo, we somberly saw all the memorial crosses along the Rio Grande River, those that lost their lives crossing the border, trying to seek a better existence. I may not have understood the complicated relationship between the U.S. and Mexico any better, but I felt a sadness indicating some things are wrong and need to be improved.

I kept returning to Mexico, each time getting more comfortable there, despite the fact that my Spanish wasn't getting any better, and the drug war was getting worse. The border has the vibe of a war zone, but the hills are *tranquillo*, in small towns locals smile and wave, a universal language.

Each time I get back to the United States after being in Mexico, something that was once old is again new. Sometimes it's the grandeur of our grocery stores, other times it's the realization that I won't have to bribe the police if I'm pulled over. Occasionally, it's noticing that our Jesus just isn't as sexy as the Mexican Jesus.

I appreciate the land we live in more with each visit. On those long drives home, headed north through the flat desert of Texas into New Mexico, I've tried to imagine what it would be like to make the decision to enter the U.S. in search of a better life, or to improve my economic status to provide for a family. As time goes by, I know I could have that question answered because I have a few friends that have lived that journey, and also several coworkers.

Someday I'll ask, but for now I just wonder. I'll wonder about a former coworker, a dishwasher who lived and worked in the U.S. for six years away from his family. As a longtime dish diver myself, I studied the guy, and found him to be the most Zen of all divers, working 60 hour weeks, always with a positive attitude. Despite my terrible Spanish and his broken English we became friends, and our conversations usually involved *cervezas*, *chicas* and *mota*. Now he's back in Mexico, reunited with his family and hopefully reaping the rewards of his hard work.

I've yet to do any more international travel beyond Mexico, as a creature of habit I just return again and again. I'm in love with the limestone and mysterious nature of the country, and still scared of its unstable and unpredictable tendencies; standing close enough to dream, yet still escaping soon enough that some of the darker realities never quite sink in, walking that fine line between tourist and traveller.

This piece was originally published in the Durango Telegraph.

15 FEMALE DIRTBAGS, THE MISSING LINK

There are many sacrifices and struggles to live the dirtbag life, but my major gripe has always been women; there are not enough of them within the dirtbag culture. Many nights spent at campfires within various climbing areas, where the men outnumber the women five to one, support this complaint. However, that all changed when I moved to Durango.

Durango is an anomaly of mountain towns, because there seems to be an even ratio of men to women that are interested in the outdoors. Typically, mountain towns seem to attract more dudes than ladies, but not here. We've got beautiful women of all types who ski, boat, climb, bike, hike and camp in the great outdoors. And, over the last few weeks, I've interviewed a few of them, to get their take on dirtbagging it in Durango and beyond.

Kat and I had been playing phone tag for a few days before I finally tracked her down. She would either be working in the field for a week at a time, or out on an adventure in the wilderness somewhere. She's an avid rock climber, who lives out of her truck, and works as an outdoor educator. Originally hailing from Maryland, the 23 year old fell in love with the dirtbag lifestyle after working at a camp in New Mexico, followed by an internship with Outward Bound. She openly expresses the happiness and joy she's found through committing to a life in the great outdoors.

"I'm definitely a dirtbag," Kat says. "I could have definitely pursued a career path where I made more money, but I'm really happy with the life I live."

For Kat, her climbing experiences led her to living the life she does. "I've never done anything that makes me so focused and in the moment all day. Once I tasted that, there was no turning back."

As a woman, she also feels that it is easier to *get away* with some of the techniques used. "People just don't expect it from the ladies. It's a thrill to live on the fringe of society."

Kat described one instance where she unknowingly ended up sleeping on a farmer's property in her vehicle, and he discovered her. "He was really angry until he realized I was an innocent, young woman. His family ended up inviting me in, and making me dinner."

Like many women in Durango I've talked to, Kat enjoys having outdoor adventures with other ladies. "It's very empowering, and there's less ego than with men."

Ultimately Kat feels the dirtbag lifestyle allows her to transcend into a higher state of freedom and consciousness. "There's just something about defying the set pattern of society. My independence from living as a dirtbag unlocked a door of personal freedom and what is best for me."

Even at the ripe age of 23, Kat realizes that women are less likely to live in a dirtbag fashion for as long as men do. "All women should start dirtbagging when they are young," she advises.

My roommate and landlord, Renee, is another local woman who could be considered a quintessential female dirtbag. She's lived out of her truck with her boyfriend Andrew, climbing and camping all over the United States.

"For me, being a dirtbag is all about forsaking money for the purpose of a dream and being able to travel," Renee says.

She's also incredibly creative with her resources, partaking in dumpster diving, and knitting her own gifts and clothes. She and Andrew have several chickens and an elaborate garden that supplies food in the warmer months. She's incredibly generous, and when they lived along the river trail last year, she would give zucchinis to strangers.

At 25 years old, Renee is quite young to be both a dirtbag and a homeowner, but she plans to use the house as a way to provide income through renting and still be able to travel and climb.

Like Kat, Renee feels a strong bond with other female dirtbags, "I grew up in Southern California, and didn't get along with other women.

I just thought it was me and then I moved to Durango and met so many rad chicks with similar interests."

Renee also feels the women of Durango, and other various mountain towns, are forging a new identity of a western woman. "When you hear stories about the wild west and mountain people, it's almost always the story of a mountain man. The mountain woman is still emerging to define herself."

Of all the dirtbags I've interviewed for this column, my new friend Rose has been the most elusive. Initially she was excited to be interviewed, but then began avoiding my phone calls to meet up. When I saw her at a get together, she apologized for blowing me off, and just said she didn't want her name to be in the paper. She finally agreed to an interview when I told her we could use a different name to protect her identity.

Rose, who is 32 years old, has lived a life of dirtbagging and adventure. She's climbed and traveled to Africa, China, India, Nepal, Egypt, Turkey, South America and Mexico. While in Africa she climbed Mt. Kenya and Mt. Kilimanjaro, and has also done big rock climbs in the Black Canyon. Among her occupations have been: waitress, barista, nanny, landscaper and house sitter. For her, the dirtbag life has always been about reducing expenses, avoiding rent, and then spending all the money on adventures.

Rose especially values her adventures with other women, especially those that are strong and independent. "Women can tend to be insecure, and it is great to find those that are not like that. My friends and I can do things that really strong men can do, and that is really empowering. We use our time in the outdoors together to catch up as well. The women I do stuff with in the outdoors are also more flexible, polite and accommodating than some men I've climbed with."

While Rose has already seen more than many people will in their lifetime, her journeys now are more inward. She tries to focus more on relationships and being grounded. Along with this, she feels her outdoor experiences, though less frequent, are richer.

"I enjoy climbing more now. I don't equate my performance with who I truly am," she says. "Just focusing strictly on outdoor activities isn't going to make me a happy person."

Rose has lived in Durango now for nine years and says she never expected to stay here so long. Part of the reason she has stayed is the community, people who strive to live a healthy, balanced life. "We grow up later here in Durango. There's not as much societal pressure to live in a certain way like there is in other parts of the country."

As for the future, Rose strives to maintain her physical fitness and pursuits, build a career and strengthen relationships with those that are important to her. "I feel like you really can have it all in Durango."

This piece was originally published in the Durango Telegraph.

16 POKER NIGHT

"You don't have TV? How do you live without TV?" my uncle asked in disbelief. I was back in the Midwest, and, as usual, something about my Colorado lifestyle was surprising my relatives. Typically the topic of conversation is about me sleeping on a rock face, or how I meet women when I'm living out of a vehicle, but this time it was my lack of access to cable.

Yes, I have all but abandoned the recreational pastimes I grew up with, with one notable exception, poker. I learned to play poker with my uncles in Illinois, and over the holidays every year we'd sneak off into a basement filled with antique beer cans, a pool table and a card table. I almost always lost my five dollar buy in, but liked the excitement of playing, and when I was old enough, I enjoyed the beer my uncles provided.

Sometime after I moved west in the late 1990s, poker blew up in popularity. In particular, Texas Hold Em, a seven card variation of poker, took the nation by storm, and suddenly it was *the way* to play the game. Even in the small corner of the world that I was living in at the time, Gunnison, everyone playing poker had adopted Texas Hold Em and there was no turning back.

Somewhere in the middle of this, I had a friend who had a grand idea: we could fund our climbing trips by gambling. He had a system for several ways of winning money with roulette, blackjack and poker. For a brief minute, I believed in his system when I won seventy dollars in thirty minutes playing blackjack in New Mexico, after returning from a climbing trip to Mexico. "See, seventy bucks can last a week in Mexico," he said.

I shared his passion for this idea briefly, until I lost two hundred dollars at a roulette table using his system. "Just keep betting on black," he said. "Eventually you'll win your money back."

Well, I kept betting on black, and the little silver ball kept landing on red until I was out of money. I still never lost faith in his idea until he left me hanging in Las Vegas one time. He was planning on meeting me there to test his systems in Sin City, but couldn't make it, something about a tooth falling out because of his frequent tobacco chewing habit.

What we didn't know at the time was there actually was a man who funded his climbing trips by gambling. For over twenty years, John "The Gambler" Rosholt was a climber by day and professional poker player by night. He funded a dirtbag climbing lifestyle from playing poker and was known for his methodical, scientific approach to both poker and climbing. Rosholt considered poker a science, and a job rather than a game. Not only was he successful with poker, but he was also one of the top climbers of his time.

Sadly, in 2005 Rosholt went missing in Las Vegas. The media covered his disappearance, and his sister Jane tirelessly searched for him. Many theories existed about his whereabouts until 2010 when a climbing party found some human remains on a wall in Red Rocks, a climbing area near Las Vegas. The remains were tested and found to be Rosholt's. Apparently he was scoping out a new route on the wall and slipped, falling to his death. There are many interesting stories about him online, and hopefully, someday, someone will write a book about the man they called The Gambler.

In Durango, I've found a great group of guys to play poker with. Like me, most of them don't want to lose more than five to ten bucks a night, and laughter is of equal importance to winning hands. My buddy Travis, a smooth southern gentleman, is the ringleader and last winter somehow convinced six to eight people down in his frigid basement once a week for a friendly game of cards. Good beer was always on hand, and it had a similar vibe to playing with my uncles, but instead of the antique beer can collection on the wall there was a Wu Tang Clan poster.

I can't overstate how cold it was in that basement. One night my friend Tim, who doesn't have an ounce of fat on his body, and suffered frostbite as a teenager, showed up in a puffy coat and pants that one might see in a picture of someone climbing Mt. Everest. Though we made fun of him, he insisted it was the only time he was warm enough down in that dungeon.

This winter Travis is off to exotic travels with his lady, but we've still kept a decent crew together. We play every couple of weeks, and have found a warmer location than a seedy, dark basement. We miss Travis and his wit, "I don't want nobody to get shot or stabbed down here, it's only poker," he would often say, but don't miss the fact that he usually won and took all of our money.

Through poker night I've met some climbing partners, new friends, and grown closer with others. It's a good time even when I lose my money, which is most nights, but I'll admit it is much more fun when I'm winning. I don't have the keen sense that John "The Gambler" Rosholt must have had, although his lifestyle was envious, and I'm glad there was someone out there living that dream.

I don't have any regrets about leaving behind a more sedentary lifestyle back in the Midwest for a more active one out here. After all, if I stayed in the Midwest I'd never have any of these stories. But, I'm glad I've hung onto at least one pastime, poker night.

This piece was originally published in the Durango Telegraph.

17 CRIMINAL KITTY AND SHEEP AT LARGE: THREE YEARS OF HOUSE SITTING

Elizabeth had just moved to Colorado, and we'd just started dating. On her third day we were both hungover from sharing some cannabis edibles, and had to meet with a couple who wanted us to house sit for them.

House sitting doesn't encompass this though, does it, I thought to myself: a yurt with no electricity, a cabin with barely any electricity, four cats, a dog, forty sheep, two roosters, twenty chickens and two donkeys. The lineup of animals, and the immediacy of sharing a space with someone I just started dating should have tossed up two red flags. But it didn't. And, why didn't it? Why was moving every month and watching strange animals for strangers becoming normal?

Midway through the tour of the property, Elizabeth sat down and nearly fainted. The couple, new sweethearts themselves in their fifties, said kind words and got her a cup of water. We played her sickness off due to the altitude, and continued on with the tour, which ended with, "Sure we'll watch your house for a month."

My adventures into full time house sitting began with the downturn of the economy around 2009. My full time job in higher education was cut to half time, and my new supervisor and I weren't seeing eye to eye. So I resigned, and decided I'd write full time.

I moved from Gunnison to Durango, with no plan other than I didn't have a plan and I wanted to write, and I'd rely on the kindness of strangers, and climbers would be my friends. Gunnison to Durango is a common transition, people get tired of the Gunny cold, or lack of jobs, or lack of *whatever*, and they move down south a few hours.

My one connection was with the local independent weekly newspaper. They said I could write for them. It would pay a hundred bucks a story. I was making thirty thousand plus benefits in Gunnison when I was full time. On paper I was doing the stupidest decision for my career I could possibly make. But, should a writer write for paper, or should he put his hopes and dreams onto paper?

So, the paper let me run a simple classified ad for free.

Responsible but unemployed dirtbag writer looking to lounge in your house and water your houseplants and maybe pet a cat. Working on the great American novel. References available from important people.

That wasn't exactly the way it read, but that was what I was thinking. Go big or go home right? I was in Joshua Tree, California, on a road trip when I got the call: *Would you like to watch our home for the winter while we're off in Mexico?*

Yes.

Do you have references?

Sure, how about the president of this college, or the editor of the newspaper? Perhaps the governor? Let me try his office.

That won't be necessary. Come by in two weeks when you're done climbing.

I was bluffing with the governor; sure I'd met him a couple times over the last few years, and maybe I'd be able to get ahold of someone at his office who remembered me, but it made me realize I was no longer a mere dirtbag. I was a person who had shouldered responsibility for three years. And responsibility begets responsibility. True, I was unemployed with nothing but a three hundred dollar, graffiti-ed car to my name, but dammit I had a resume.

Like Superman, I could go into a booth and change from dirtbag to responsible thirty something. With that, I went from a guy living out of his car on a road trip to a new resident in the great city of Durango who lived by himself in a three hundred thousand dollar house in a subdivision.

House sitting is merely a higher level of couch surfing. I'd probably spent a year of my life surfing couches. All for the dream of climbing. With couch surfing and house sitting, the code of ethics is basic: be respectful, clean up after yourself, and make yourself wanted. Be such a good couch surfer your host would rather have you there than not. Same with house sitting: take care of the house, the plants, and the animals; make yourself valuable.

When I was couch surfing, I lacked ambition to do anything that wasn't climbing. Now, after my three years of a 9-5, I had ambition; I had a burning desire to work, and more importantly to write. Once I was in Durango I scoured the classifieds every day looking for a job that could utilize my skills. I applied, went to interviews, met with the president of the college and other important people. I thought I'd have a job within a month. I didn't get one. When I lowered my standards to jobs that paid the same as what I was making in college I still couldn't find work. A shot in the heart. Was this what Bob Dylan meant when he wrote *twenty years of schoolin' and they put you on the day shift?*

But I couldn't even find a day shift.

Luckily, I was able to get unemployment insurance: a couple hundred dollars every other week, to get me by. A lot of people talk shit about other people on unemployment, but it was saving me, and I'd paid into it for sixteen working years. I was one of those people on unemployment who actually wanted to work.

My drive. I don't really know where it came from. I think it was my thirties. All throughout my twenties I had passion, but not enough discipline. I'd get fired up about some environmental or social issue, but would rarely follow through. I'd just go climbing. I put so much damn effort into climbing. Too much effort. Now climbing is the spice of my life, but before it was the main ingredient.

Without a job, but with the fire, I just woke up every morning and wrote. I wrote for hours, fueled by coffee, and that human desire to get your story on paper. Get that story recorded and then it outlives you. Be a part of something bigger. Inspire people. Make them cry. Make them laugh. Make them feel sorry for you. Make them feel envious. Be human, and put all the victories and mistakes into a story.

For some reason I could write and write in that house, and everything just flowed. Maybe it was the setting: a south facing solarium that created natural heat and allowed sunshine in just perfectly, a wide open ceiling that went up for thirty feet to a fan that circulated all that warm air, an elegant middle class kitchen with proper dinnerware and a feeling of sophistication, a bookshelf with classics from Hemingway, Fitzgerald, and Garcia Marquez. If I were feeling sorry for myself I'd just look around. I poured it all out onto the paper and at the end of a writing morning I felt damn good about myself. And, I still had all day to do whatever. I'd never been so free. More importantly, I was working, and freedom without meaningful work is nothing for a thirty-something, its purgatory really; freedom is an ingredient, another spice of life.

My chores were simple: vacuum the floor, clean the bathrooms, shovel the snow, and keep the houseplants alive, basic stuff. There weren't any pets. I could leave for a couple days at a time if I wanted. I had an extra bedroom for guests. This was The Greatest House Sitting Gig In The World.

Day after day I wrote stories from the great dirtbag experiences of my life. I read books from their bookshelf. When I got tired of the house I'd go running or climbing, or write more in the coffeeshop. I was a little lonely, being new in town and all, but I was a climber and a climber always meets other climbers. It's one of the greatest things about climbing, if you're a decent human being you'll never run out of friends.

Word was out that I had a house in Durango and guests came through. One of those mysterious dirtbag laws of the universe: have a couch to offer and they will come. I had dinner parties, and we lived it up in this strange, magical juxtaposition. When spring arrived, and the owners of the house returned, I cleaned that place leaving no counter unwiped, no toilet unscrubbed and no carpet unvacuumed. They were pleased with my efforts and promised to call me again if they ever left for another winter.

I hit the road for Yosemite. With nothing lined up in Durango, I went back to the Gunnison Valley after the road trip. It was purgatory. I partied too much, and wrote too little. I had a good summer with friends, but my drive was beyond having a good time like it was in my twenties. After the summer, I'd return to Durango. I ran another ad in the paper and scored another house sitting gig. This time in addition to loafing and watering plants I would watch an animal, a dog, a sweet deaf white dog named Asha. Her owners would be off in Myanmar doing humanitarian work for a month. I liked the idea of being part of that, even in a very minor way, and I had a month to figure out my living situation in Durango.

There I was again, in another nice middle class home, living by myself, with an exquisite office to compose my words in the morning, with only slightly more responsibility: walking the dog. Asha roamed free most of the time, but demanded her morning walk. She woke me up at seven every morning barking, saying, "It's go time." I started my coffee and walked the dog, and then I wrote.

Before they left, the owners of the house told me a neighbor was looking for a hand with her horses. It would pay like ten bucks an hour. Still collecting unemployment, I figured I could use a couple bucks cash on the side, so I inquired. It turned out the work was horse mucking, a proper way to say cleaning up horseshit. Maybe a year before I would have declined, but I was getting more humble by the day. So I mucked.

It actually wasn't too bad. It only would last for an hour or two. The woman was really nice and had a brother who was a rock climber who had passed away at a young age. Maybe something in me reminded her of him. When you get along with someone its amazing what you'll do for them. And, after Interim Director of the Office of Public Relations and Communications, Assistant Director of Public Relations and Communications, and House Husband in Training, my resume could now list Horse Mucker.

This is where I started to get into trouble. Everything went well for the month, and once I got used to Asha's morning walks (I prefer to do nothing but drink coffee and write in the morning) the dog and I got along famously. Then other calls started to roll in. One guy in particular I agreed to meet with because he was a climber. He had a place in the hills, completely off the grid, solar powered, small farm, with many farm animals. A kind of sustainable, if the world goes to shit kinda place you'd want to probably live at, because you would survive longer than you would in a modern home with nothing growing to eat, and completely locked into the grid that is the modern American existence. I was intrigued.

The couple had me over for a homegrown dinner at their property, which was thirty minutes from town, off the highway and then twisting and turning for several miles on dirt roads. They served me a hearty meal of veggies and meat. After dinner, I got a tour. There were solar panels that provided electricity, a wood stove, a backup generator, marijuana plants, a greenhouse full of vegetables (even in early winter), chickens, pigs, horses and a fat cat. There was even Internet access. It would be my modern day Walden for a month. Another piece of the puzzle to get locked into Durango, this place I wanted to call home, but had to find a way.

I was a year into my unemployment streak. I was hardly depressed by the situation, maybe I should have been, but I just kept writing and climbing, and that usually keeps me from depression. And then I was secluded by myself in this cabin.

It was February in a dry winter thus far. My little car made it up the winding dirt roads to the cabin, but they left a big diesel truck for me in case the car got snowed in. The routine in the morning was like this: wake up, make coffee, start the generator, fetch some wood and start a fire. Feed hay to horses, feed pigs their grains (they would even eat horse shit if you threw it in their pens), check on the couple of chickens, feed kitty, go back inside and write. Write for a while and then water the plants in the greenhouse. There were several water collection tanks, and I liked the idea of this existence: be responsible for your food, water and shelter.

Each day I would make the thirty minute commute into town. I didn't have to do it everyday, but I did have to do it everyday. I couldn't imagine a day going by and not talking to someone, seeing someone. Even if it was just going to the coffeeshop, or to a yoga class. The thought of a day all to myself, secluded in a winter cabin, was terrible.

And then it started to snow. And so I shoveled the snow: off the house, clearing off the solar panels. My car was stuck up there, and so I used the big diesel truck. Even though a round trip to town cost me twenty bucks in that beast I still made the drive everyday. I was lonely.

One day the pigs got loose, and I chased them around before they finally went back in their pens. They were filthy beasts, but it didn't hinder my affection for the taste of bacon. The hay from the horses made me all stuffy and sniffly, and hay was all over my clothes all the time it seemed.

I thought my writing would flow being up there all by myself, and I managed to get some words onto paper, but it did not flow as a spring river like I hoped. Predicting when art will happen is like predicting the weather or when you'll fall in love. I tried.

It snowed and it snowed, and there I was all by myself in the cabin. One day after my trek to town in the truck, I was climbing up a snowy road, and the diesel was humming along. I was on autopilot, thinking all I had to do for this day was get to the cabin, and I'd be chillin' for the rest of the night. Then, I looked up and ambling down the snowy road was a propane gas truck headed straight for me. Fuck.

Despair. I was going to die The Saddest Death of a House Sitter Ever. He was coming right for me with a tank full of propane for a head on collision in a vehicle that I didn't even own. Suddenly at the last minute he swerved to the side of the road, barely missing me. He smiled when he finally drove past. I hated him for that smile. I was terrified, and sick to think that I was born into a world where I could have died a death like that.

I was counting down the days at the cabin like a school kid ready for summer. And, I was ready for spring. I learned that spring comes quick in Durango, compared to many other mountain towns, and soon I'd be hearing the birds chirping, women would be all about wearing less clothing, flowers would be blooming and rocks and sunshine would dominate my days.

The second to last day before it was over the truck broke down while I was making my rounds to town. I spent the night at a friend's house, and then called the owner in the morning. He suggested I get back up there before the horses got restless and decided to take off. *Dammit this is a job*, I thought to myself. *And, what am I doing it for?*

So I hitchhiked, and it was like all classic hitchhiking rides: a guy picked me up who had dated a girl who was from my hometown, and he was a climber who had also lived in Crested Butte. There were all of these nuances and synchronicities that came into play and it brightened my spirit. This was why I loved rural Colorado because you could hitchhike and rely on the kindness of strangers from time to time, and everyone has stories and your stories intersect just like your paths do together. He dropped me off and I just hiked up the rest of the way that differed from where he was going. I was finally back at the cabin, and all of the animals were still there, hungry, but still there. Then I decided that I was overextending myself, and I needed to start charging for my house sitting services. Right after my next one, with more plants and animals, two minutes from town, right next to a local climbing area.

Maybe *this* was The Greatest House Sitting Gig Ever. I moved from the cabin in the hills to a great modern middle class palace just minutes from town. From dark and secluded to open and sunny. The owners were nearly my parents' age, but a hip version of them. They were going backcountry skiing in British Columbia for the month. The first thing they said when I met with them, "This is Sparky, our dog. He's old, don't worry if he dies."

They also had a murderous little kitty, named Kitty, who pounced on mice and birds. There were a dozen chickens, with a well tended to coup. The garden was still put to bed, being barely spring and all. A few hundred yards away was East Animas, our sandstone crag that can match up with local crags anywhere. At the last minute they told me, "Well, our friend Mark was going to stay here, he's going to be coming through on a book tour, but we'll be gone. Bummer."

I inquired more and told them I'd be happy to let Mark crash at the place. At this point I'd only met a few true authors, and they were who I wanted to be. Turned out Mark had written this book called *The Man Who Quit Money*, and the focus of the book was this gentle, modern vagabond named Daniel, who, in fact, refused to use money. It was a bit of an indie hit at the time, and I was beyond curious. "Please, demand that Mark stays here," I pleaded.

After we discussed Mark and Daniel more, we realized we had mutual friends, who had mutual friends with them, and in turn we were mutual friends. And then, officially, I realized if I had mutual friends with people who were my parents' age then it was destined that I was going to be a grownup at some point in the near future. I finally knew what I wanted to be when I grew up: I wanted to be like these people who I was house sitting for. Have a couple animals, a nice little sustainable house, a lover, a garden, and a charmed life in this little town nestled between the desert and the mountains called Durango.

So, still unemployed, I lived a month there in complete happiness. I met friends up at the crag to climb the sandstone, and finally found some sort of balance there. It's one of those crags no matter how hard you climb the holds seem to be facing the wrong way, and the gear is strange, and all of a sudden you're scared out of your mind, climbing on another planet, and all you want to do is get back to the ground on planet Earth. But then you attune yourself with your surroundings, and you put in your time, going through the grades, climbing the classics and then you're home. And, then you're in the moment, and you just assess the dangers and risks one by one, and something beautiful happens and you can't explain it in words unless you were John Long or Jack Kerouac.

With all this energy in me, with spring in the air, fully blooming, I found myself a project. *Chingadero*. It means something like fuck or shit in Spanish, and I'm sure I uttered those words a hundred times working this route: a fifty-foot line of crimps and tiny, tiny footholds that required balance, finger strength, and persistence. A hold had recently broken off, and there was much talk amongst the locals that it had been bumped up a grade.

One day, while trying it, a fire built within me, and I simply had to send it that day. As I reached the crux, and began the crossover, while gently tiptoeing around the holds, I fell. And then I screamed, and I screamed so loud everyone at the crag heard me, and it echoed as far as an echo could go, and my belayer said, "Easy buddy, reel it back in." The beast was alive.

And in all men lives a beast that must make peace with the man. At that moment, on that particular crag, with the sunshine beating down, the world was perfect, and I was lucky enough to be born into this world. When I started to calm down and breathe, the beast was released. The snow capped mountains to the west smiled, and my home for the month was just down the trail.

This Kitty, he was a little murderer, and I loved him. He was the runt of the litter, a tiny little cat, all black, who loved to kill. Each and every day he would drag a mouse or a bird into the house. I was okay with the murdering of mice. I don't like mice and there always seems to be more than enough of them in the world. Sure, I'd spend ten minutes each day cleaning up the remaining insides of a mouse, but that was my job. The bird murdering was a little more difficult to stomach. Kitty would wound the bird, bring it in, and then let it fly around, destined to die, but still thinking it had a chance. Kitty would hurt it more and more, and then just pounce on it, and drag it around on the floor. Eventually the bird would die, and I'd have to clean it up. Not cool Kitty.

Mark, the writer, and Daniel, the man who doesn't use money, arrived in the middle of this blissful month, with some of my mutual friends from Gunnison. They were on book tour. Man, if I could ever go on a book tour that would be about The Greatest Thing In The World, I thought to myself.

When they arrived at the house I was out climbing, and they dropped some things off, most notably some pastries left on the counter that had clearly been day-olds, or dumpster dived; obtained for free, for sure. They left for the book presentation, and I was planning to make it, but I stayed out climbing until the sun went down. I went to bed early, and everyone came in while I was asleep.

In the morning there was a house full of interesting people, and what is a nice house without guests? My friends from Gunnison also knew the folks I'd house sat for before this gig, the one up in the hills, and everything felt very interconnected and synched. Those moments in life where you feel like you're on the right track and everything is going to work out.

Mark seemed the groggiest, after all he delivered a presentation the night before at Maria's Bookshop, and from what I heard it was one of the most well attended all year. While he made his morning tea, I started asking him questions with the pace of a first year newspaper reporter. *"How many other books have you written? Did you self publish? How long did it take you to make it as a writer? Have you made it, I mean do you make a living just writing? Why didn't Daniel write the book, I hear he's a writer? How many more stops on the tour are you doing? What advice do you have for me?"*

He answered politely, and dipped his teabag in the tea, looking at me groggily. I calmed down a bit, I mean I was a writer too; I was just a writer who had not yet written a book, which in a way seems like being a virgin. I could write, but I did not have that fat piece of proof, that printed book that declares once and for all, if I accomplished nothing else in my life I did this, and it wasn't all for nothing.

After my barrage of questions, everyone gathered in the living room. Daniel emerged from his room, and he seemed like a quiet, gentle spirit, even if he survived on discarded pastries. We all planned to go to breakfast, my favorite breakfast joint, The College Drive Café. And then I got worried how Daniel would pay.

We waited. Don't all great breakfast joints have that necessary wait? Where you're hungry and maybe hungover and all you want to do is eat, but you have to wait. Daniel asked questions about me. He lived in Moab, and asked if I ever considered living in Moab. I told him I loved the town, but didn't care for Mormon culture, and in Utah you can never get away from Mormon culture. He lived in a cave. He worked but refused payment for his work. He lived on karma alone.

We had breakfast and Mark simply picked up the tab for Daniel. I mean Mark was making money off this book about a man who didn't use money, so in karma terms it just worked out that Daniel would get his breakfast paid for. Things just worked out for Daniel. They gave me a copy of the book, for free, and both signed it. I read it in a fever, and wished it was longer. Mark was in tune with Daniel's spirit.

After this dream gig, I decided to start charging for my house sitting services. Animals are work, and more and more people were calling me asking if I did shorter stints: watching their house and pets while they were away for the weekend. I moved into a house, paid rent, and just started doing weekend gigs for a little extra money. My unemployment ran out and I got a job at a Mexican restaurant. It was far from ideal, I'd made thousands more per year with my public relations position, but my writing dreams were kept alive.

There were dream gigs, which usually involved nice, like-minded people, with well behaved pets, sweet gardens and hot tubs. Then there were strange, animal people. Like "crazy cat lady" who paid me ten bucks a day to go over to her house, feed her fat cats, and water her plants. She had a special device that measured the moisture level in the houseplants, and accused me of not properly watering them when she returned home. There were also a couple of "crazy chicken ladies". One said, "my chickens are like my pets" and another suggested I cuddle with her favorite chicken, once a day for five minutes. I turned down both of those gigs. Close relationships with chickens are the house sitting version of a red flag.

Months later I returned back to my original gig in Durango. The owners were headed back to Mexico for the winter. By then my first book was published, I was a virgin no more. The house had the same feeling and flow. It had now been two years without a girlfriend, plenty of girls, but no girlfriend. At the end of the winter I got reacquainted with Elizabeth, a woman I'd met in my last summer back in Crested Butte. She was visiting from the East Coast and had a boyfriend when I met her. I pined over her for a month afterward and we stayed in touch through the guise of writing and climbing, two passions we shared.

Eventually she broke up with the boyfriend, and had moved to Chattanooga, Tennessee, a part of the south that is renowned for its climbing. She loved the dirtbag climbing lifestyle, and wanted to take it further, to move out West. We started to correspond, and I fell in love with her words. She was in the East, desiring the openness and freedom of the West, and I was in the West, desiring a woman to come into my life. She suggested moving to Crested Butte; I thought that was a good idea, then she suggested moving to Durango, even better, I said. Then she asked if she could stay on my couch. Damn. Spring was here and my heart was open. I wrote her hand written letters. We replied sweet nothings over email, and talked on the phone for hours.

And then, Elizabeth set off for Colorado. Just over twenty four hours later she arrived on my doorstep, like the answer to a dream. She was groggy when she arrived, and I was on my way out to work, so I told her to make herself at home. And I meant it. When I came home from work that night she had rested and was doing yoga. She was as beautiful as I remembered.

We talked and played Scrabble and then I made a move. She said she thought I was shy and gentle and this side surprised her. We had an innocent night listening to soul music, and savoring the promise of new love.

The next night I had friends over to meet her, and we ate some cannabis edibles. Too much. Paranoia, then dizziness. A terrible, terrible second day. And, in the morning we had to meet up with this new potential house sitting gig.

In hindsight, I could tell it was poor judgment from the beginning. She would start the house sitting gig while I finished up mine, and then I would live there until I found a place to live. With fifty some animals, she could surely use the help.

Two weeks after Elizabeth arrived, I went to Mexico for a wedding. She dropped me off at the airport. She'd started the new house sitting gig, and was already in love with the West. When I returned she picked me up; having a lover waiting for you at the airport is one of the great joys of life.

I joined her at the property. It messed up my writing routine, and when my writing routine is out of whack, I become irritable. Plus there were all these animals to attend to: chickens, sheep, cats, dogs, donkeys and the llama. I had to start a generator just to use the computer. The honeymoon was over. I just wanted my own space back, and it was gone.

There were moments of despair, being too close for comfort, but we kept it positive. I moved into my own place, so we could have space to grow our love. We took a road trip to Yosemite. She was a great co-pilot. We talked and talked and told the stories of our lives. We made love in tents, climbed rocks and ran trails.

When we returned, she went up to Crested Butte for a weekend. I agreed to stop by the farm and feed the animals. One of the sheep had escaped. With his crazy slanted eyes he looked at me. I looked back. He did not want to run away, but he did not want to be captured.

I chased that sheep around for an hour. Just when I thought I had him corralled back into his pen he would run faster, and cut back in the opposite direction. I gathered some buckets and chicken wire, trying to create a blockade where I could get him.

I was frustrated. I cursed at that slanted eyed beast; he didn't know what he wanted. And, maybe neither did I. What was I chasing? Why would I move so many times in this new town that was slowly becoming home? I'd lived in fifteen different places in two years. Did I have a plan, a focus, or was I just moving around, out of instincts, to live and eat another day? And was there anything wrong with that? I was tired of it; I knew that.

And I finally got that little guy, wore him out, forced him into my blockade, grabbed him by the collar, and put him back into his pen.

And then, it was pretty much over. My writing picked up, and I went on book tour. I found an affordable place close to downtown, and told all my house sitting clients I was retired. My relationship with Elizabeth fizzled, not destined to go the distance, but rather to have some sweet stolen moments at the end of a crazy period in my life.

But the leap worked. I am at the place in my life where I hoped to be: writing my mornings away, telling my stories. I have a job that allows me to eat, and a community of people to climb, run and laugh with.

I see the people I've house sat for around town, and we small talk like people do. With each person I see the memories come flooding back. The plants and animals I cared for, the strange nuances of their properties, and the people I distanced myself from because I did not want to see what they were like when something went wrong.

Durango is where I want to settle down. I felt drawn to the landscape immediately after my first visit. And now I'm drawn to the people and the culture. When the time comes to buy a place, I've already seen many of the options of property and housing, and styles of living. Someday I'm sure I'll purchase a place, with a lover, maybe have a cat and a dog, and if she wants them, maybe kids. And, eventually I'll probably need a house sitter of my own, and inevitably some transient looking to make a few bucks, or just in need of a place to crash for a while, will answer an ad in the newspaper. And maybe I'll see a part of my former self in their eyes, and if so I might start off with something like, "You know, I used to do some house sitting myself."

18 JUST THE FOUR OF US, THE BROMANCE

Romance is an essential part of life, the story of the world revolves around it, and many great men have fallen to their knees for a beautiful woman, and vice versa. Love makes us strong and it makes us weak. Thus, there are thousands of novels about it, and even an entire genre, The Romance Novel. I want to take it one step further, and introduce The Bromance Novel.

As I'm writing this, the computer program is underlining bromance, not recognizing the term. Silly computer. It's okay though, Microsoft Word, bromance is a relatively new concept, and I forgive you.

Bromances are beautiful because you can have many of them at the same time. No one is going to get jealous. You could start a bromance on the trail, at the bar, or even on the street. It's a connection thing: the recognition that you are a dude and so am I, as pure as the kid looking for someone to play with in the neighborhood. We men are simple creatures, and unlike a romance, your potential partner in bromance isn't likely to analyze you to no end upon meeting. He just wants a buddy, and you can never have too many buddies.

A couple weeks ago, fresh off of a breakup with my last girlfriend, I was in need of some serious bro time. Fortunately, three of my best buds were in need of the same. It was Tim's birthday, and a Sunday, which is the day we try to set aside to go running for our unofficial and nonexclusive Sunday Running Club. An unusual morning rainstorm was ensuing, but instead of bailing we rallied and headed up to the mountains.

We packed up my Subaru and drove toward Engineer Mountain, our objective for the day. Tim was turning 37, and he wanted to commemorate the day with athletic feats, plus a multitude of high-fives, which I'll get into here shortly. Long gone are the days of binge drinking to celebrate birthdays, we prefer endorphins.

I swear my car already started to smell the minute four dudes packed into it. We'd yet to break a sweat, but somehow an air of dude overcame the entire confines of the Subaru. On the drive up, we chat about our relationships, and offer advice. Most are on the prowl, while I'm reeling from a breakup. My homies hear me out, and I appreciate them for that. The bromance meter is ticking up.

The rain continues to pour. We could bail, but the bromance level would dip down, so we throw on some rain jackets, strap up our running shoes, put our man pants on and start jogging up.

The rain alternates between drizzle and downpour, yet we march on. We speak in the language of bromance: shouting, laughing and farting. An hour into the run and we are close to the summit. Two weeks ago we were shut down by bad weather, and it happens again. It was not our day for the mighty Engineer Mountain. Jonathan has summit fever but we talk some sense into him. "It's not a time for heroics up here buddy," Al says, persuading him to go down by sweet talking him into getting some grub at our favorite breakfast joint.

Back in my car we are muddy and sweaty, and the stench of my car already equals a weeklong road trip. Ewwww…downfalls of the bromance. We beeline it straight to breakfast, and get our name in for the expected twenty minute wait. While loitering in the parking lot, we decide to do pushups. Tim cranks out 37, and then high-fives us. Only 34 more high-fives to go.

We take a *siesta* at Jonathan's, watching the latest climbing movies, cultivating some man-crushes. "Alex Honnold, so hot right now," Al says. Honnold is the star of the climbing world right now. He climbs stuff without a rope that we can't even do *with* a rope. His *National Geographic* cover shot, and an appearance on "60 Minutes", has solidified a level of stardom that no rock climber before him has attained. We also watch a film about Himalayan alpine climbing, where they smoke cigarettes at night in a portaledge (a hanging tent used for climbing) to curb their hunger. Bromance taken too far, if you ask me. We encourage Tim as he cranks out 37 pull-ups and 37 sit-ups.

It was time to complete the high-five challenge. Off to City Market, and we spread the stoke of bromance. Tim approaches strangers for high-fives, and every single one smiles and obliges. What a town! With his 37th high-five of the day the mission is complete. What do we do now? Go rock climbing of course. The rain has subsided and there's nothing more bromantical than a multi-sport day.

After dangling on overhanging limestone during a slight drizzle, we are spent, and retire downtown for dinner. Tim's Birthday Challenge is complete, and Jonathan says he feels like he just had a weekend getaway in his own town. The beauty of Durango baby!

We all go our respective ways, you can't take the bromance home with you, but you can take home the memories. Socks, shoes, and all sorts of disgusting remains get left in my car, and I spend a week airing it out and trying to find the proper owners of said filth.

There are downfalls of the bromance for sure, which reminds me that these days of bromantical bliss won't last forever. I'll find romance again, which will take time away from these sweet nothings of bromance. And, maybe someday, when I'm older, hopefully as a writer-househusband who takes care of the cat, dog and houseplants, I'll record more of these moments into a best selling bromance novel.

This piece was originally published in the Durango Telegraph.

19 K-BONE, A LEGEND PASSES ON

Last month I wrote an article on bromance, which, as it turns out, has been the most popular article I've ever written for the *Durango Telegraph*. How do I know this? People have been stopping me left and right to tell me they enjoyed it. On the street, in coffeeshops, and where I work, the original version of the Facebook "like" - compliments in person.

I'm not sure how to take this because I've always thought I'd make my mark as a writer by writing about important issues. Before and after the bromance article, I wrote in the *Telegraph* about the drug war in Mexico and a film about photographers in Afghanistan. The feedback I received on those pieces was miniscule compared to the bromance article. What to take away from this? I really don't know. Maybe when people pick up this paper they'd rather laugh than cry; maybe we get enough information about wars and depressing situations that we'd rather read about something fun going on in our backyard. I'm just speculating, like I said, I don't know.

I know I write for you, so I want to deliver. The words are mine for a minute, writing can be therapy, but once they are printed they are yours.

Right now, as I write now, my heart is hurting, and my stomach has been in knots since I got the news. My friend, Kevin Volkening, aka "K-Bone", was killed in a climbing accident last week in Clark's Fork, Wyoming.

In fourteen years of climbing, he's the first friend I've lost to the pursuit, a statistical miracle, given the dangerous nature of the beast that is climbing. I know I should not be alive today from some of the mistakes I've made while climbing. While telling a friend about the loss recently, he described climbing as something that involves high risk and huge dividends. I couldn't agree more.

But a loss isn't about numbers, or words, it's the tears you cry, and the tears you know those who are much closer to him are crying. The ache in your heart that you'll never see him again, and then knowing he has a wife, parents, sisters, a grandmother and many other loved ones that have a void in their hearts bigger than any canyon.

My time with Kevin was extremely limited. I met him through some mutual friends in Salt Lake City, while visiting for the bi-annual Outdoor Retailer Trade Show. He'd just started working for Black Diamond, and we hit it off immediately, mostly due to his welcoming nature. We shared a love for Indian Creek, and he joked that he thought all Colorado climbers were douchebags until he met us. He was the kind of person that could throw out an insult like that because you knew immediately he was so loving at heart.

He wore his "spirit shirt" every Friday, a howling wolf, and the last time we talked he told me he had over a dozen of them. Even at the Outdoor Retailer (OR) show, when most of us were dressed in some of our finer duds, Kevin would wear his wolf shirt. He stood out as a bright light of a human being. At the most recent OR show we met his wife, Marge, and they were obviously in love and very happy.

It takes a very special person to make you feel like you're friends immediately upon meeting them. Many of us, myself included, let our insecurities or fears get in the way of our true selves. When he died, Kevin was a new friend of mine, one I hoped to spend many days climbing with, especially in our beloved Indian Creek, where there's little but red rock and red dirt, our cell phones don't work, the climbing is difficult, but living in the moment is easy. We were just planting the seeds of friendship; my heart knew we were kindred spirits, and now I know after reading about him he had that impact on many other people.

From his obituary in the *Lewis Tribune* newspaper I found these words, "Kevin had the ability to bring out that deep down hidden kindred spirit within each person he met and to share that spirit with others. Such was his way to make the world a better place for everyone."

From that obituary, I also learned that his hunger for adventure began young. At 17 years old he and his father rode their bicycles from the Pacific Ocean to Chicago, covering more than 3,000 miles in 45 days. A longtime Bozeman, Montana climber, he also climbed all over the country, including the big walls of Yosemite and Zion. Much of his college work at Montana State University focused on the changing climate and glaciers, and he made several trips to Alaska.

In the wake of the death of a loved one, we are forced to examine our own lives. I feel drawn and determined to be the best person I can be, and to put forth my best effort with my projects and goals. Tomorrow is never guaranteed, but with today we can live in the moment and give everything.

Often I feel like I'm running on a treadmill of life. I think that's why climbing and other outdoor pursuits are so rewarding. They force us to live in the moment, and remind us that the greatest joys of life are the simple, challenging things.

And death reminds us of something too. It's sad and terrible, and if that person is close to you, you may never be the same, ever again. My heart is going out to the people who Kevin lived close to. May their spirits be lifted of the fond memories, and may they know that Kevin was a bright light in an often dark world, and his legend will live on.

This piece was originally published in the Durango Telegraph.

20 LOST

*"The same thing that makes you live
Can kill you in the end."*

Hank to Hendrix by Neil Young

whaaaaaaaaaptt

"What was that?" one of us asks.

No one can answer what the loud popping-snapping noise was. It's too soon for hunting season, so probably not a gun. We keep running.

Our "run" is actually a combination of running and fast hiking. We are doing a lap up Engineer, the most popular moderate mountain around Durango. On most days there's a full parking lot of twenty cars, and fifty hikers on this trail. Today it's just us and a handful of other people.

It's rainy and cold. A fog surrounds everything; we're a few hundred feet from the top, but can't see the summit. The calendar says summer, but fall is certainly in the air, with a hint of winter. It's always winter somewhere in Colorado.

My eye is on my brother when we leave the trail, and scramble to the top. Loose wet rock, with a steep drop off. He's a married man, visiting from New York City. Clint's life is beyond his life, and his life is in my hands. Jonathan wants to go the top. I am hesitant because my brother is with us. Tim is patient and waits to see what everyone decides. Tim is always patient.

Sometimes for the sake of adventure you have to go for it. So, we go for it. We scramble on the third class ridge like climbers. My brother scrambles like an athlete, but not a climber. You can tell a climber by the way they use their feet, delicate and precise. The drop off is covered in fog. How far the fall would be is shrouded in a milky layer of cloud. I imagine if he did slip how I would stop him?

Fuck

Fuck

Fuck

How did this happen? We made it through the technical, slippery finish, and here we are four hours later, lost. Wet and lost. Wet and lost and cold. Clint is finally worried. I've been worried ever since we lost the trail, and started down this drainage. Fours hours later we are still in the same drainage. It's so cloudy I can't even tell where the sun is. We have nothing but the wet clothes on our backs and one small water bottle.

We haven't stopped moving ever since we decided to start down this drainage. I thought it would take us back to the trail. We lost the trail in a momentary lapse in concentration. We've crossed the icy cold creek maybe thirty times, zigging and zagging, back and forth. On the inside I'm full of fear, doubt and dread. On the outside, my words are calm, collected, encouraging that with each crossing of the stream we're getting closer to the trail, the road, something.

I hope we're headed to the highway, but we could be headed deeper into the wilderness. Night is approaching, and all I can think about is the three unplanned nights I've stayed out in the wild. But, I always had layers, and it was always dry. You never know how big the price is for a simple mistake until you have to pay it.

The Beach Party

I see Clint once or twice a year. When we were kids we used to fight everyday. As the older brother I teased him and beat him up, until at 15 he started playing football and lifting weights, and I was no longer stronger than him. Then, a peace treaty of sorts was signed, we finally became friends.

In higher education we took two different paths: he ended up earning a law degree in Chicago, while I studied at a liberal arts college in the Rocky Mountains. Now he's a lawyer in New York City and I'm a writer in Colorado. We get along famously, and I cherish every

118

moment with him. On paper we are different, in the heart we are the same.

This is his first visit to Durango, and I want to show him the flavor of my new home. Yesterday it was a zip up to Telluride, where we went to a going away party at a "tiny house" for a local celebrity. We camped in his front yard, awakening to waterfalls, mountains and cool, fall morning air. It's always winter somewhere in Colorado. After a quick breakfast we blaze back to Durango. We're throwing a beach party at the Golf Wall. It's almost always summer somewhere in Durango.

We often describe our beloved little chuck of limestone known as the Golf Wall as hanging out at the beach. The hands of God oriented it to be a solar center, and with the minimal effort it takes to hang out and lounge in the sun, well, it feels like the beach. A decent percentage of my life is spent in this leisurely state. It's what keeps me young.

I call Clint my younger older brother, because, well, he is. He's got more salt and pepper in his hair, is more responsible, and generally lives like an adult. I'm chasing a dream with a lifestyle that matches a twenty something. Clint knows how to have fun though, and he's loving the Beach Party. We've got beach balls, squirt guns, a cooler full of drinks and fake mustaches. I was hoping for girls in bikinis, but apparently we didn't get the word out properly. Next year.

Most importantly, Clint connects with my friends. He trades good natured insults, and gets a taste of the funky climbing culture I've been telling him about for years. At the end of the day only one of us is sober enough to drive. We leave my car at the parking lot, and pack seven of us into one car. And, the next day we plan to retrieve it after hiking Engineer.

An epic begins with one mistake

Mind at ease, body hungover, we're past the technical difficulties. Jonathan and Tim up ahead in the distance, out of sight because of the fog. Clint and I jog along; another thirty minutes and we'll be out of this cold, wet rain and back to the car. But somehow we lose the trail. I swear we were just on it.

The trail is gone. We retrace our steps, moving a few hundred feet to the right, and back to the left. Like vapor, the trail has disappeared. We can't see the top of the mountain to regain our bearings. Neither one of us has our cellphones to call Tim and Jonathan, or look up our positioning on a GPS. Clint looks to my expertise. I spot a drainage, "Let's follow this drainage down, it should lead us to the lake halfway down."

So we go. Immediately I'm worried. Clint is not. He trusts my judgment, but all of a sudden I don't trust my judgment. Long ago when I was on a mountain rescue team I remember someone saying, "If you're lost, just follow the drainage down, it has to lead to safer ground below."

So we commit to the drainage. With each passing minute the fear inside slowly builds. "We're wet and cold and lost," my inner guide says. My outer guide directs Clint, "okay, let's be careful here," as we cross the stream from one side to the other. He's clueless about my dull, but piercing fear. We cross the stream so many times I lose count. I'm praying for the sight of the road. An hour goes by, two hours, three hours, four hours. We are still hiking down the drainage. Soaking. Clint is fearful by now, out of that basic human fear for being cold and so far from warmth and shelter.

This is the single greatest adventure my brother and I have shared, I think. And it may lead to a night in the wilderness, wet and cold, and probably leading to hypothermic conditions. But I must be in the moment as we tip toe across the stream again. A broken ankle would be the worst thing in the world.

I step on a rock that shifts under my weight, to another that does the same. I must balance, and take care. Clint follows. We move swiftly along the riverside. The one piece of technology we have, the time. Clint looks at his watch and updates me, the later it gets the more worried I am. I wish I knew for sure that we were headed in the right direction. The sun is buried in fog, and has been all day. I just hope we're headed to that great highway, instead of deeper into the wilderness. The buried sun is our only source of light; we don't have a headlamp, or even a lighter.

Finally, finally, after four and a half hours in this drainage, of being lost, we come across signs of civilization: a small hunting camp next to the river. This is good, I think, this is something. I express this sentiment to Clint, confidently. Inside I think about the nights I've spent naked to the world, out in the wild, unplanned, without a sleeping bag, stuck on a rock face, climbs that took two days instead of the planned one day. They were transformational experiences, shivering under the stars of the night with good friends. Two men huddled together out of sheer necessity. One time we were so cold we wrapped our ropes around our bodies, and shivered. But we were never wet. We were always dry. Cold, but dry, little danger of hypothermia. And here we are, the night approaching, wet, wearing shorts, and no idea where we are.

We have to take that hunting camp as a good sign. Ten minutes later we see another, a rusted can of beans in a long abandoned campfire. And then fifteen minutes later, another: a hanging rack for a killed deer or elk. Twenty minutes after that, a bridge, a bridge! There's a forty foot limestone wall, and a small waterfall, and that bridge.

"We have to be close to a road," I exclaim. Spirits are higher. And we run. And we are running for our lives at this point, the very essence of running. The running that was running before it was a sport. Neither one of us has taken a sip of water for five hours. Clint has never even been on a "mountain run", something I've been doing for years. He's not adjusted to the altitude. But, he's crushing it. I'm proud of him, but at that moment I can't be proud, I can only expect. Expect that he can continue this performance, until we find our way. And then I start to think I know where we are. Cascade Creek. And, like the thought of being proud of my brother, I can barely process, I think about Jonathan and Tim, searching for us…

They waited at a meadow just down the trail. A place where we usually meet up. We didn't show up. They hiked back up to look for us. And saw us. Phantoms. It was not us. They ran all the way down to the parking lot. They drove up and down the highway. They went back to the parking lot. Worried.

Then Jonathan ran back up, again. And then he remembered the noise, we heard earlier in the day:

121

whaaaaaaaaaaaaappt

It was a gunshot, the first victims. And we were next. Fear overcame his psyche; he could be running into his own death. He was okay with it, *if this is how I go, this is how I go.* But nothing, no one, not us, not anything but a deep mysterious lingering fog. The sun was going down. He yelled and yelled for us, but nothing.

And we are immersed in that same fog. The joyous buzz of running is wearing off, not a sign of civilization or humanity on the trail. I think I know where we are, but it's just an inclination. Maybe hope. Are we going to spend the night out in the cold with nothing to protect ourselves from the elements?

We ran for three miles on that trail that we hoped would lead us to a road. For fifteen years I've been trying to get away from society, to get closer to nature, and now all I want in the world is to see a sign of humanity. I've never been lost before. Never. I've read reports about how people get lost and analyzed them and found their mistakes. I worked in mountain rescue and looked for hunters who were lost and I thought I was better than they were. I've climbed the tallest cliffs in Colorado and California and thought I was an experienced outdoorsman, that I had something figured out. I am humbled to the core, and all I want to see is a house, a person, a road. Anything.

After those three miles I suggest we turn around. Clint does not argue, but his confidence in me is waning, he's worried now, I can tell. We're both worried. So we run back. We continue to run for our lives, but there is no more joy, only survival. We pass the bridge by the waterfall again. I scope it out. That would be where we would go when the night came. We would at least be protected from the rain. We would get cold and huddle together, like I did before on the rock walls.

And then we come to a fork in the trail. There is a fire pit by it, and a tree that kept the area dry. This would be where we would stay tonight, I think again. I vote to go right on the trail, up the hillside, maybe it would lead to something. Clint suggested we go the other way, left, into a meadow of green, skirting the hillside. I go with his instinct. I am the experienced Colorado mountain man, but my judgment is clearly off. I got us lost. We go left.

Damn, if we weren't lost this would be a beautiful moment with my brother. All of my best friends, our bonds have been cemented by defining moments in the wild. When we trusted our lives to one another, and we emerged, different, that after the experiences we were somehow better for it. All around was the majestic beauty of Colorado that saved my life so long ago, that gave me something to live for. Now, it's all up in the air, will we survive this night out in the open?

I look to my left, across the river, and there are limestone cliffs and waterfalls. The waterfalls run for hundreds of feet down the cliffside. And what do those limestone walls look like up close, I wonder, barely. Someday will I return to this trail in a reflective state of mind remembering that day we got lost?

We run, and then we see smoke. A sign of something! As we get closer we see it's an outfitter's tent, with a wood stove billowing out a healthy stream of smoke. A legitimate structure. We approach the tent with the desperation that two lost people have.

We catch the couple off guard. "Sorry to bother you, but we're lost, we started the day on Engineer...do you have a map, or could you tell us where we are...?"

I am too desperate to feel ashamed. And then I take stock of my surroundings.

There's a pie, no wait a cheesecake, a no-bake cheesecake.

I take in a deep breath and smell the cheesecake, and the burning wood, and I know we will be okay.

They are calm, and helpful, some unspoken code that people in the outdoors will try to help one another. They get out a map. They show us where we are. We were running in the wrong direction. We were a mile from the road when we turned around. They give us a headlamp. I promise to return it, but they refuse. They saved us.

We run joyfully again, past the bridge; I look at cliffs and waterfalls and promise myself to return and retrace these steps. We are in Cascade Canyon, a beautiful, little limestone paradise. Our hips and legs ache, but we continue to run, past the point where we turned around, and then there's a house. And another house. And we're happy.

We find the dirt road and come to the highway. We stick our thumbs out to hitch hike. In a minute, a truck stops. It's a couple in their forties and the woman has a bouquet of flowers in her lap. They were returning from Crested Butte, my old stomping grounds. On the radio is Blackalicious, one of my favorite hip-hop groups. It's cosmic and they're nice. The woman lets me borrow her phone to text Tim. I have his number memorized from the days before I had a cell phone. He texts right back, and I sensed the relief in his words. The couple drops us off at my car, parked by the Golf Wall, from the beach party the day before. My keys are in Jonathan's truck. We sit and wait in the cold until Jonathan and Tim show up. A few empty, cold, yet relieved moments.

Over dinner we discussed our errors, and I told Jonathan and Tim the experience was probably worse for them. While terrifying for us, we at least had the control of knowing. They had no idea what was happening. They would have called a rescue team to start searching for us in the morning. I felt bad and humbled, but more relieved than anything. Tonight we'd sleep in beds, and we would be warm and happy.

The next day, sore and exhausted, the sun was out again. We went climbing at a local crag that overlooks town. It was hot and we basked at the base of the rocks. It's almost always summer somewhere in Durango.

It was one of those days where climbing is not the main part of climbing. I set up a toprope for Clint, and he still had the energy and gumption to climb. I was proud. We talked about the previous day and tried to bring it to life. It was the past already. Today was all bluebird sunshine. But, my brother and I had a great adventure, and we had a story. I had been lost, truly lost, for some hours, and that humbled me.

I'm in my mid-thirties, more fit than I've ever been, the prime of my existence for endurance sports. The deep lust and hunger of my twenties is replaced with a small inkling of wisdom that knows pure enthusiasm often gets you into trouble. And, now I know just a simple run you've done before can turn into an epic, especially when you're in the wild. Maybe it was complacency that got us into trouble? Maybe it was not opting to bring a phone, or a headlamp, or even a lighter? The lesson of this experience will stay with me, I hope.

When I was younger, I climbed for my soul. Now, I also run for it. I know a truth in my life: I need to have great experiences in the wild to be who I am, to self-actualize. What was a terrifying experience, wondering if I'd just got my brother into more trouble than we'd ever been in our lives, has turned into a story. The more alcohol, the easier the story is to tell. He told his wife, and then we told our parents, and over the holidays Grandma got to hear it. Our greatest adventure ever together as brothers. And we survived, together.

I wanted to retrace those steps this fall, but winter's blanket of snow came and covered it up. Spring is in the air now and the white of snow will soon be replaced with dirt. When that happens, I'll lace up my running shoes, and head up into that canyon to revisit those waterfalls and limestone walls to see if they are like I remembered them. And remember, that first time, I was lost.

ACKNOWLEDGEMENTS

I chose not to do a detailed acknowledgments section with this book. Last time I did and ended up leaving out a couple notable people in my life. If that was you, know I love you, and it was not on purpose.

Instead of naming people, I'd like to just thank my friends, family, climbing partners, lovers, editors and teachers. Through writing these books I've learned success is always a team effort, and I promise to pay it forward to the next generation, with the good karma that has been sent my way.

ABOUT THE AUTHOR

Luke Mehall is a born again dirtbag living in Durango, Colorado. He is the publisher of *The Climbing Zine*, an independent print publication and website, and the author of *Climbing Out of Bed*. He is a proud graduate of Western State Colorado University in Gunnison. He enjoys climbing, runs in the park, gluten free beer, hip-hop, yoga and uninterrupted mornings of writing. Luke loves hearing from readers and can be contacted at luke@climbingzine.com.

Check out more of Mehall's writing at:

climbingzine.com

lukemehall.blogspot.com

48806399R00080

Made in the USA
Lexington, KY
13 January 2016